GCSE ENGLISH 2

Writing &
Coursework

RHODRI JONES

JOHN MURRAY

Acknowledgements

Copyright material is reproduced by kind permission of the copyright holders: Eileen Fairweather and The Women's Press (Livewire) London 1987 (p. 11), British Rail InterCity (p. 20), David Higham Associates Ltd (p. 25), Ray Bradbury and Hart-Davis (from *The Golden Apples of the Sun*) (p. 26), Flair (pp. 29–30), Laurence Pollinger and the Estate of Frieda Lawrence Ravagli (pp. 36–7), Ralph Glasser and Chatto & Windus (pp. 45, 68–70), Graham Greene and The Bodley Head/William Heinemann Ltd (pp. 50–2), Valerie Avery and Thorsons (pp. 55–6), Edward Blishen and Penguin (pp. 57–8), Gerald Durrell and Grafton Books (p. 63), Laurie Lee and Chatto & Windus (p. 67), the estate of the late Sonia Brownell Orwell and Martin Secker & Warburg Ltd (p. 67), Melville Hardiment (pp. 71–2), Colin Malam and *The Daily Telegraph* (p. 72), the estate of A.J. Cronin (pp. 73–4), ITP (pp. 78–9), Jon Stallworthy and OUP, 'The Last Mystery' (from *Out of Bounds* 1963), Jessie Pope and *Punch*, Elizabeth Jennings and Macmillan, 'My Grandmother' (from *Collected Poems*), Norman MacCaig and The Hogarth Press, 'November Night, Edinburgh' (from *The Sinai Sort*), David Holbrook 'Unholy Marriage' (p. 83), Vernon Scannell (p. 87), Caroline St.-John Brooks and *The Sunday Times* (pp. 90–91), Doubleday (pp. 92–5), Martin Cutts, Chrissie Maher and Allen & Unwin (p. 99), Barnet Press (p. 101), Duckworth (p. 107), Norman Longmate and Chatto & Windus (pp. 108–9).

Photographs are reproduced courtesy of: Robert Estall (p. 27), Sally & Richard Greenhill (pp. 59, 65, 75), Michael Pattison and *The Daily Telegraph* (top p. 84), *The Guardian* (bottom p. 84), Philip Wolmuth (top p. 85), Bob Gannon (bottom p. 85), Spanish National Tourist Office (p. 96).

© Rhodri Jones 1989

First published 1989
by John Murray (Publishers) Ltd
50 Albemarle St, London W1X 4BD

Cover illustration by
Sebastian Quigley/Linden Artists
Typeset by Phoenix Photosetting, Chatham
Printed and bound in Great Britain at
The Bath Press, Avon

British Library Cataloguing
in Publication Data

Jones, Rhodri
  GCSE English
  2: Writing and coursework
  1. English language. Writing skills –
  For schools
  I. Title
  808'.042

ISBN 0–7195–4667–2

Contents

Introduction

Writing and Coursework is the second book of *GCSE English*, a complete GCSE course. The other books are *Reading and Understanding* and *Oral Communication*.

In *Writing and Coursework*, you are guided through various skills necessary for you to acquire if you are to write effectively and produce coursework that represents your best work. These skills range from choosing the right tone and an appropriate language to developing ideas and selecting the best words.

Many examples of written material are provided for you to examine and analyse – short stories, extracts from novels, newspaper articles, advertisements, descriptions of people, places and events, letters, directions, explanations and instructions. By studying these, you should be helped to an understanding of what makes effective writing and should be able to carry this over into your own writing.

GCSE English requires candidates to demonstrate their ability in a range of writing situations. The advice given here and the practice suggested should help you to produce effective writing of different types and to the best of your ability, such as is required whether you sit an examination as part of your course or are assessed solely on coursework.

Each section of the book looks at a specific writing skill or a particular aspect of writing and provides material which enables you to examine this skill or aspect in detail. The book is divided into two parts. The first is concerned with matters that affect all writing. The second indicates approaches to particular kinds of writing and suggests assignments for coursework, marked by the symbol ◆.

The book is based on a close examination of the National Grade Criteria and the syllabuses of all the GCSE examining groups.

Part One

Looking at General Aspects of Writing

1◆Appropriate Language

Suppose you were asked to write each of the following:

a personal account of a family celebration

the minutes of a school council meeting

an essay about the Welfare State.

What kind of language would you use for each? Would it be the same in each case? Would it be formal or informal? What kind of language would be appropriate?

Standard English

This is the most formal kind of language. It is the language used by the majority of educated English-speaking people. It is the kind of language used in formal situations and is grammatically 'correct'. For example:

> Under the arch of the main entrance the heat and light struck at one like a blow. For a moment Anita was blinded and stopped, steadying herself against one of the stone pillars of the wide veranda, until her eyes adjusted. Formal trees surrounded the circular driveway, which was of white sand brushed ten times a day by one of the gardeners, and her view of the main gate and the enticing world that lay beyond was hidden by a great fountain.

Monica Hughes, SANDWRITER

Colloquial English

This is less formal. It is the kind of language used in everyday speech between friends. It uses idiomatic phrases called colloquialisms (for example, 'What have you been up to?'), abbreviations (for example, 'I'm' for 'I am'), and need not necessarily be grammatically standard (for example, 'There's loads of them' instead of 'There are a great many of them').

Slang

Slang is even less formal than colloquial English. (Compare Standard English 'man' with colloquial 'chap' and slang 'geezer'.) Slang expressions tend to be less widely used and understood than colloquial language. They also tend to be fashionable for a while and then become dated. Examples of slang are 'lolly' (= money), 'nosh', 'goggle-box', 'go spare', 'get lost'.

Dialect

Dialect is another non-standard form of English. It is the form of language peculiar to a particular area or social class. Different dialects are marked off from each other by differences in pronunciation, vocabulary and grammar. For example, 'brew', 'mash', 'wet', 'soak', 'mask' are all words used in different parts of Britain for making tea.

(For a fuller account of these and further examples, see *Reading and Understanding*, Chapter 1, 'Kinds of Language'.)

It is possible to use all of these kinds of language in your writing. None of them is 'better' than the other. Which you use depends on which is most appropriate.

Look again at the questions suggested at the beginning of this section. In writing a personal account of a family celebration, relaxed and informal language would be appropriate. You are giving a **personal** account. You are sharing an exciting and enjoyable event with friends. You would use much the same kind of language you would use when telling friends about it in conversation.

But would this kind of language be appropriate for the other assignments? In the minutes of a school council meeting, would it be more appropriate to write

Brian was a bore as usual, going on and on about school dinners, *or*

Brian spoke at length about school dinners?

The first version may be more vivid. It may be the kind of thing you would say to a friend or write in a letter. But is it appropriate for the minutes of a meeting which are supposed to be a formal record? Isn't it too personal and informal?

Similarly, you might use language like this in an essay on the Welfare State:

There was a right argy-bargy between the Labour and Conservative parties over setting up the Welfare State.

But would this be appropriate? You are presumably presenting an account of the Welfare State that is serious and reasoned. You are presenting your thoughts and views to a general audience for consideration. A phrase like 'a right argy-bargy' would not match the seriousness of the subject and the approach. It would jump out at the reader and jar. It would be more appropriate to keep to formal language (that is, Standard English) throughout and write

There was strong disagreement between the Labour and Conservative parties over setting up the Welfare State.

Formal language would probably be appropriate for the following kinds of writing: official letters, reports, factual descriptions of events, instructions and explanations, the narrative in a story, formal essays.

Less formal language (to varying degrees) would probably be appropriate for the following: letters to friends and relations, personal writing, the narrative in a story being told from the point of view of a particular character, dialogue.

But note: this is only a rough guide.

When considering what kind of language is appropriate for a particular piece of writing, you need to bear the following in mind:

the subject matter and the situation
the audience addressed
the purpose of the writing.

A Say what kind of language is likely to be appropriate in the following situations. Justify your view. More than one kind of language may be appropriate in some cases.

1 A letter thanking a grandparent for a birthday present

2 A review of a school play for a school magazine

3 An account of a holiday you spent with a friend

4 A story about someone playing truant

5 An explanation of how a television set works

6 An essay on the dangers of pollution

7 A description of a demonstration

8 A letter applying for a job

9 A story presented through the eyes of a pensioner

10 An essay giving your view on school uniform.

B Examine the following passages. Say what kind of language is being used in each and how appropriate it is as far as you can tell.

1

A recent page in *The Times* boosting those flash new swimming complexes that so many cities have taken to running now that they all have leisure directors instead of parks superintendents, was decidedly snooty about the municipal baths of old.

‘Gone are the days when a visit to a public pool was acutely depressing if not positively frightening. No longer is the hapless swimmer forced to shiver in the changing rooms, weep from the chlorine and cower from humourless lifeguards only too anxious to enforce the long list of rules . . .’

It makes the old Bog Street Baths sound like Pentonville Jail (‘*I sentence you to seven lengths on the first charge and five on the second, to run concurrently*’) but I’m afraid that’s not how I remember it at all.

Keith Waterhouse, WATERHOUSE AT LARGE

2

This one I'm going to tell you about, me and my mate met her in an all-night caff near the Elephant. It was when times were bad, and around midnight you always got the same sort of crowd. There'd be a few beggars off the street, hanging it out over a cup of tea, elbows on the table and trying to get a bit of sleep in without being spotted. You'd get some of the young Elephant gang in as well, wide boys, and a dirty old man or two, some brass that had come off the streets to rest their feet and have a jaw and a smoke in peace, a ponce or two, and like as not, a stranger.

Bill Naughton, THE LITTLE WELSH GIRL

3 It was my last day in the small lakeside town and the Kenyan couple with whom I had been staying suggested that it would be a good idea for me, a traveller from distant regions, to be introduced to the District Commissioner. It would, they implied, be not only a courteous gesture but a modest act of homage rendered to the new Kenya whose virtues had been loudly sung during the weekend. 'You will like the DC,' my friend's wife had assured me. 'He is one of the kindest, most honest men I know. You won't meet a more straightforward person anywhere.'

Shiva Naipaul, NORTH OF SOUTH

4
'Ain't got a spare Daisy, gal, I reckon?'
Mrs Strickland, staring with diffused and pleading eyes through the dust she had raised, groping up towards the sumptuous pumpkin of Mrs Rankin on her window sill, ran a dreary hand several times across her brow.
'Ain't got nivry one left,' Mrs Rankin said. 'You had the last one yisty.'
Daisies were a brand of headache powder guaranteed to refresh and free you from pain in five minutes. Mrs Strickland was taking them all day.
'Ain't Bill a-workin' then?'
'Bad a-bed. Can't lift 'isself orf the piller. I wisht Albie was here.'
I knew Albie couldn't be there. Albie, who was eighteen, a private too like me, was in France, fighting the Germans. I liked Albie; he had a ginger moustache and was my friend. Every other day or so I asked Mrs Strickland if and when Albie was going to become a lance-corporal, but somehow she never seemed to think he was.

H.E. Bates, LET'S PLAY SOLDIERS

C Find short passages which illustrate the use of Standard English, colloquial language, slang and dialect. Consider whether the language for each is appropriate.

D Rewrite the following passages as Standard English. Say what your versions gain and/or lose when compared with the originals.

1

The most boring place in the world
Hornsey
London N8

Sept 3rd

Dear Jean,

I know it's not my turn to write but I'll drop dead of boredom if I don't do something. If I don't die of Pneumonia first, that is.

Today I hung around the bus stop outside Hornsey High for TWO HOURS and all that earned me was a soaking. No Keith Edwards, just two hours of Hornsey rain. I'd spent hours getting ready, as well. I looked dead good, too – I'd got on Sue's black plastic jacket and that pencil-line skirt of hers that makes me look almost thin. I bust the zip but I put it back into her wardrobe before she got in from work so maybe she won't notice. I don't fancy getting beaten up by her when it was all for nothing.

God, Hornsey must be the most boring stupid place in the world. We're so far from the middle of London I might as well live up in Lancs with you. Not that Ashton-under-Lyne sounds like anything to write home about. But I'm glad you did – if only so I know I don't have to bother getting jealous. God knows why your parents had to move you 203 miles away just so you could live beside a load of demolition sites and closed-down mills. Sue's new boyfriend Derek is a travelling salesman, and he says A-u-L is the kind of place they make television documentaries about. I don't think he meant that as a compliment. Still, as your dad says, it's good for trade that Ashton's got the highest proportion of pubs of any town in Britain. I suppose people up there drink to forget.

When I came in today, I asked Mum for a swig of her sherry to warm me up, but she just swiped me one. I was only looking for sympathy, but she's hard as nails, that one.

Yours, sneezing a lot,

Maxie

PS Now I feel guilty for slagging off Mum. She's just come into my room and said that she's taken the afternoon off work on Friday so she can buy me a new uniform. AND she reckons she should have enough to buy me a non-official super-sexy PENCIL-LINE SKIRT!!!! She's been saving her tips for me all summer. She is sweet.

Eileen Fairweather, FRENCH LETTERS

2

New Year's Day gone, the morning I was sitting on my doorstep as I like to do when I got something to think about; and as I sitting there thinking about all the resolutions I could make to go through the year with, all of a sudden I notice people going down the road in ones and twos, hurrying like they going to a fire or something. Now, when a man like me see that they have something in the air, the onliest thing to do is to get up and see what happening. So I up and start cruising down the road too. I see Edgar going bird-speed in the same direction, so I ask what all this is about.

"Eh-eh! You ain't know?" he say. "Man, you missing a big bassa-bassa. Jasper and Saga-boy going have a stick-fight, because Saga-boy take Germaine to a Old Year dance last night."

Well, I know this is a serious thing now, 'cause nobody don't ever risk doing that sort of thing with Jasper. I mean, everybody know that Germaine is Jasper girl-friend and everybody know also that Jasper is a man who very cruel when he get jealous. But of course Saga-boy feel he is more sweet-man than anybody else, so he up and take out Germaine though he know what sort of man Jasper is.

Timothy Callender, PEACE AND LOVE

E   Choose one of the following subjects. Write two paragraphs about it, one in Standard English, and the other in less formal language. Comment on the differences between your two paragraphs and say which of the two you prefer and why.

1   My favourite breakfast

2   Winter

3   Nuclear power

4   The cave

5   Saturday mornings.

2 ◆ Audience and Tone

Much of what you write will be directed at people of your own age with similar interests – for example, stories, personal writing, letters to friends. But there may be occasions when you will be writing for a different kind of audience or reader – for example, writing to a potential employer, or to the local newspaper, or to your MP.

You need to keep the **audience** for whom you are writing constantly before you. It will affect the following:

your subject matter and how you treat it

the kind of language you use

the tone you use.

For instance, a letter applying for a job would be quite different in all these respects from a letter to a friend describing what you said in your letter of application.

The **tone** you use should be appropriate for your audience and your subject matter. In speech, the tone of voice we use to say something shows whether we are angry or sad or surprised. In writing, tone is indicated by the kind of words and language we use. For example, consider the following:

I am disgusted by the way I am being treated. I don't see why I should have to put up with it.

I very much regret that you have chosen to treat me in this manner. I do not feel that I have deserved it.

Both are extracts from letters of complaint, but the tone of the first is angry whereas the tone of the second is pained and hurt. Both would be possible. It depends on the writer's attitude towards the audience and the situation.

Making sure you choose an appropriate tone is important. Choosing the wrong tone could be unfortunate – for example, a letter of application for a job where the tone is arrogant, or a leaflet for pensioners where the tone is patronising, treating them as if they were children.

(See also *Reading and Understanding*, Chapters 4, 'Tone' and 5, 'Audience Addressed'.)

A How would the audience in the following situations affect the way you write?

1 A report for a local newspaper

2 A letter to the governors of the school

3 A story intended for primary-school children

4 A leaflet encouraging parents to come to a school jumble sale

5 A letter inviting a speaker to talk to your club.

B Choose a subject and write two different versions of it, each of which is intended for a different audience. For instance, you might choose 'sports day' and write a report for the local newspaper and an account of the day for your own diary.

C What kind of tone would be appropriate for each of the following? There may be more than one possibility in each case. What affects the choice of tone?

1 A personal account of your feelings about football

2 A letter of congratulation

3 A review of a school play

4 An account of a geography field trip

5 An appeal to parents to contribute to the school fund.

D Write short paragraphs illustrating each of the following:

a contemptuous tone

a frightened tone

a respectful tone

a sarcastic tone

an arrogant tone.

3◆Sentences

A sentence can be defined as a grammatical unit consisting of a word or group of words that is complete in itself. It usually consists of a **subject** (what the sentence is about) and a **predicate** (which tells us about the subject). The predicate includes a **finite verb** (a form of the verb which relates to the subject and has a **tense** – present, future, or past). For example:

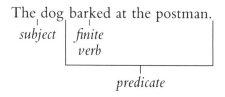

Sentences can be more elaborate than this example and can have more than one clause (that is, more than one finite verb). For example:

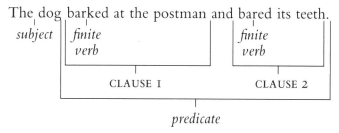

Sentences begin with a capital letter and end with a full stop, a question mark or an exclamation mark.

It is also possible to define a sentence as a statement, a question, a command or an exclamation that makes complete sense. For example:

The door is locked.

Who are you?

Go!

How dreadful!

The last example does not contain a finite verb. Sentences without verbs are possible and acceptable – for example, in answer to a question or for dramatic effect:

Will you be there? Certainly not.

He called again, urgently and desperately. He listened, straining his ears for the slightest sound. Silence.

Sentences can be short or long depending on the purpose of your writing and the audience for which it is intended. For instance, short sentences may be effective in describing tense action or when giving instructions. Longer sentences may be effective for a detailed description or a reasoned argument.

But if you always use short sentences or always use long sentences, there is a danger of monotony. Try to vary the length of your sentences according to what you are writing. For example, a short sentence after a series of long sentences can be effective as a summing up or in making a dramatic point:

> Behind him, he could hear his pursuers closing in on him, the sound of their boots clattering on the cobbled roadway. Ahead of him was the river, gleaming in the moonlight, its turbulent water cold and uninviting. There was no escape.

Try also to vary the pattern of the sentences you use. Different types of sentences are:

the **simple sentence**, consisting of one statement—for example:

> The rain beat against the windowpane.

the **periodic sentence**, where the thought is developed until the main point is reached at the end—for example:

> Although she went on wheedling and coaxing and used every trick she knew of to get me to change my mind, I remained firm.

the **balanced sentence**, where one idea or statement is balanced or weighed against another—for example:

> Some people may enjoy lying in the sun, but I prefer to sit in the shade.

the **loose sentence**, where phrases or statements are added to each other in a rambling kind of way—for example:

> The house was in a poor state of repair, with peeling paint and crumbling brickwork, and loose tiles hanging from the roof, as though no one had bothered to do anything to it for years.

A Examine the sentences in the following extracts and comment on their effectiveness.

1

As soon as I got to Borstal they made me a long-distance cross-country runner. I suppose they thought I was just the build for it because I was long and skinny for my age (and still am) and in any case I didn't mind it much, to tell you the truth, because running had always been made much of in our family, especially running away from the police. I've always been a good runner, quick and with a big stride as well, the only trouble being that no matter how fast I run, and I did a very fair lick even though I do say so myself, it didn't stop me getting caught by the cops after that bakery job.

Alan Sillitoe, THE LONELINESS OF THE LONG-DISTANCE RUNNER

2

A wave of anger went over him: anger against himself for blundering into this mud-trap and anger against the land that made him feel so outcast, so old and stiff and stupid. He wanted nothing but to get away from it as quickly as possible. But as he turned, something moved in his eye-corner. All his senses startled alert. He stopped.

Ted Hughes, THE RAIN HORSE

3

The sudden removal of the Prince was not merely a matter of overwhelming personal concern to Victoria; it was an event of national, of European importance. He was only forty-two, and in the ordinary course of nature he might have been expected to live thirty years longer. Had he done so it can hardly be doubted that the whole development of English policy would have been changed. Already at the time of his death he filled a unique place in English public life; already among the inner circle of politicians he was accepted as a necessary and useful part of the mechanism of the State.

Lytton Strachey, QUEEN VICTORIA

4

> Dad was very hot on mental attitudes. And diet. And sleep. In fact on practically everything that had to do with running, even in the most indirect way, even when it came to what I read, what films he thought I ought to see. As for television, he wouldn't have one in the house. Well, not for years, anyway.
>
> *Brian Glanville,* MY SON THE RUNNER

B Give your own examples of the following:

1 Three sentences, one of which does not contain a finite verb

2 A sentence that is a statement

3 A sentence that is a question

4 A sentence that is a command

5 A sentence that is an exclamation

6 A simple sentence

7 A periodic sentence

8 A balanced sentence

9 A loose sentence

C Write two paragraphs, one consisting of short sentences and the other of longer sentences. Make sure in each case that the kind of sentence you use is appropriate to the subject matter and the audience for which it is intended. For example, your paragraph of short sentences could be outlining dramatic action or describing strong feeling. Your paragraph of longer sentences could be a description of a scene or a detailed point in an argument.

4❖Paragraphs

Most pieces of writing are divided into sections called paragraphs. Each paragraph deals with a particular thought or idea and should be to a certain degree complete in itself. A new thought or a new idea should have a new paragraph.

Each paragraph begins on a new line and is indented from the margin. (In some print and in much typing, as an alternative, a space is left between one paragraph and the next.)

Using paragraphs can help you to present your ideas in a logical and orderly way. It can help readers to follow the events or the argument more easily. The pause at the end of one paragraph enables the reader to have a moment's thought to take in what has just been read before moving on to the next paragraph and the next point.

Paragraphs can be short or long – a simple sentence or a whole page. The choice will depend on the purpose of the writing and the audience for which it is intended. For instance, a series of short paragraphs may help to carry the reader along from point to point. Longer paragraphs may help to develop a point or a description more fully. But too many short paragraphs may break up the writing too much. Too many long paragraphs may hinder the reader from following the line of thought.

Varying the lengths of paragraphs can be effective. For instance, a short paragraph containing a single sentence after a longer paragraph can alert the reader to an important point or can be dramatic. For example:

> The house was in total darkness. The moon bathed it in a blue light and cast the shadows of the tall trees across the lawn. There was no sound except for the whispering of the leaves as the wind ruffled through them.
> Slowly, Tony edged forward.

When planning a piece of writing, it can be useful to note down the main idea or topic of each paragraph. These ideas can then be incorporated in the paragraphs as **topic sentences**, that is, sentences which indicate what each paragraph is about and which the paragraphs illustrate and expand on. The topic sentence is usually the first or the last sentence of the paragraph. For instance, in the following example, the first sentence is the topic sentence:

> Karen was always in trouble. If there was a disturbance in the playground, she was sure to be at the centre of it. If a class was noisy, she was sure to be shouting louder than anyone else. If there was a mob on the staircase, she was sure to be leading it.

Linking words and phrases can be used to move smoothly from one paragraph to the next and help the reader to follow the line of thought. Some examples are 'however', 'on the other hand', 'in addition', 'alternatively', 'nevertheless'.

A Examine the paragraphs in the following examples. Comment on the effectiveness – or otherwise – of the paragraphs.

1

Do seat belts restrict your thinking?

Somehow you can't quite imagine Albert Einstein mulling over a mind-bogglingly brilliant concept strapped into a plane with a pre-packed lunch on a plastic tray.

Or Wolfgang Amadeus Mozart composing his Horn Concerto in E flat in a car in a contraflow.

Can you picture a tycoon planning his next take-over whilst overtaking in the rain?

Some forms of transport, it seems, are just not conducive to constructive thought.

Consider an alternative. Consider InterCity.

First Class passengers sit relaxed watching Britain whizz past at up to 125 miles per hour.

They order food and drink from attentive waiters.

Briefcases snap open. Reports, pre-viously rendered incomprehensible by jangling office phones, suddenly make sense.

Someone scribbles figures on a scrap of paper, devising a budget with tax at 20 pence in the pound. (We should be so lucky.)

Someone else attempts to recall Arnold Palmer's 18 best golf holes in the world.

Crosswords are cracked, often in record time.

A brilliant response to Karpov's latest opening gambit comes like a bolt from the blue.

People catch up on their reading, go for a stroll or formulate strategies. They arrive feeling fresh, relaxed, more alert.

Their minds have been stimulated, sometimes by doing nothing.

Makes you think, doesn't it?

ADVERTISEMENT FOR BRITISH RAIL INTERCITY

2

He was near the sea now, flying straight over it, facing straight out over the sea, over the ocean. He saw a vast green sea beneath him, with little ridges moving over it, and he turned his beak sideways and crowed amusedly. His parents and his brothers and sister had landed on this green floor in front of him. They were beckoning to him, calling shrilly. He dropped his legs to stand on the green sea. His legs sank into it. He screamed with fright and attempted to rise again, flapping his wings. But he was tired and weak with hunger and he could not rise, exhausted by the strange exercise. His feet sank into the green sea, and then his belly touched it and he sank no further. He was floating on it. And around him his family was screaming, praising him, and their beaks were offering him scraps of dog fish.

He had made his first flight.

Liam O'Flaherty, HIS FIRST FLIGHT

B This passage was originally printed as four paragraphs. Divide it again into four paragraphs and justify the divisions you make.

First of all, you have to make up your mind about the subject of your collection. The world is yours and the choice is unlimited. But you certainly have interests in some direction already—dogs, or carpentry, or embroidery, or aeroplanes, or drawing, or gardening. My own collection of dog's-head whistles in wood, metal, ivory, and bone was started because I have three dogs of my own. My wife, who is an expert needlewoman, has brought together, piece by piece over the years, a very fine collection of fittings from old sewing-boxes—mother-of-pearl silk-winders, miniature tape-measures, silver needle-cases and so on. After making up your mind on a subject, you must be ruthless in your policy of discrimination. If you are interested in drawing and decide to collect, say, Victorian prints, you cannot leave it at that. There must be millions of Victorian prints. There is no fun in amassing great piles of paper in this way, and of course it would be impossible from the point of view of cost alone. Say to yourself something like this: 'I'm interested in cats—particularly Siamese cats. I'll look for early steel-engravings of Siamese cats. I wonder when the first Siamese cat came to England anyway, and how? I might find a print showing the first one, and I'll have a date to work from then.' This is the way a true collector thinks. You'll probably go to the local library and get a book on Siamese cats which will tell you when they first appeared. You'll become a member of the Siamese Cat Club (there must be one) and find another collector of early steel-engravings. You'll write to your fellow-collector, and find you both have duplicates which you would like to exchange. This is just an example to show what I mean. You may loathe Siamese cats, but the principles are exactly the same whatever your interests are. One of the amazing things I have learned through my odd collections is that no matter what you collect, someone else in the world collects it too. All you have to do is find him.

Christopher Scott, COLLECTING FOR FUN

C 1 Write two consecutive paragraphs, the first consisting of three or four sentences, and the second of a single sentence. Make sure your paragraphs are appropriate to the purpose of the writing.

2 Write a paragraph containing a topic sentence. Underline your topic sentence.

3 Write two paragraphs where the line of thought is carried over from the first to the second by the use of a linking word or phrase.

D Write paragraphs, one for each, in which the following are topic sentences:

1 The whole performance was exciting.

2 There is no doubt that dogs make good pets.

3 The landscape was rich and varied.

E Write down the main ideas or topics for each paragraph for a piece of writing on one of the following subjects:

1 A day by the sea

2 Why I enjoy or dislike television

3 Playing truant

4 The advantages and disadvantages of supermarkets

5 Fear.

5◆The Best Words

Coleridge the poet described poetry as 'the best words in the best order'. Whether you are writing poetry or prose, you should try to use 'the best words'. This means using the words that are most appropriate for your purpose and the words that reveal what you are writing about in a fresh and interesting way. Here are some aspects of words you should keep in mind when you are writing.

The colour of words

Different words have different shades of meaning. For instance, in describing a character you might use the word 'thin' or 'skinny' or 'slim'. 'Thin' would suggest a neutral statement of fact. 'Skinny' would suggest a contemptuous or comical degree of thinness. 'Slim' would suggest something elegant and something that is being approved of. You have to choose words which have the right 'colour' or bias so that readers can gain the impression from your writing that you want them to have.

Figurative language

By using figurative language you can often convey your ideas in a more interesting and effective way. The two main devices in figurative language are the **metaphor** and the **simile**. A metaphor is a comparison in which we say one thing is something else or has the qualities of something else which cannot literally be the case. For example:

Linda has a grasshopper mind.

A simile is a comparison in which we say one thing is like something else. For example:

Linda has a mind like a grasshopper.

The plain literal statement would be

Linda can't concentrate on anything.

By expressing this idea in the form of a metaphor or a simile, a stronger impression is conveyed. The reader has a picture of how a grasshopper jumps from one spot to another and can associate that with the way Linda's mind works.

Meaningful words

Use words which precisely convey the meaning you want. For instance, compare the following

Andrew walked up the road.   Andrew sauntered up the road.

Andrew trudged up the road.

'Walked' is a flat statement of fact. It gives the reader no clue as to **how** Andrew walked, whereas 'trudged' and 'sauntered' do.

Adjectives and adverbs

These can also help to convey your meaning more precisely to the reader. For example, compare the following:

> The lane disappeared into the distance.

> The **narrow rutted** lane disappeared into the distance.

> He called out.

> He called out **threateningly**.

Do not use too many adjectives and adverbs or the effect can become cloying or monotonous.

Sentences

The kind of **sentence** you use can help your meaning to be more effective. (See Chapter 3 'Sentences'.)

Active and passive verbs

Verbs can be active (the subject is performing the action) or passive (the action is being done to the subject by someone or something else not necessarily specified):

> Mary cut the grass. (active)

> The grass was cut once a week. (passive)

Using an active verb gives a more immediate effect. Using a passive verb is more impersonal. Choose the one which best suits your purpose.

Repetition

Repeating words or phrases or patterns of words can help in achieving particular effects. For example:

> Slowly the boat floated down the river; slowly the grassy banks drifted by.

But be careful to repeat words like this only when a particular effect is intended.

(See also *Reading and Understanding*, Chapter 6, 'The Colour of Words', and Chapter 7, 'Figurative Language'.)

A Examine the words used in the following passage and say how effective they are in creating the impression the writer wishes to convey.

It was six o'clock on a winter's evening. Thin, dingy rain spat and drizzled past the lighted street-lamps. The pavements shone long and yellow. In squawking goloshes, with macintosh collars up and bowlers and trilbies weeping, youngish men from the offices bundled home against the thistly wind—

'Night, Mr Macey.'

'Going my way, Charlie?'

'Ooh, there's a pig of a night!'

'Good night Mr Swan.'—

and older men, clinging on to the big, black circular birds of their umbrellas, were wafted back, up the gaslit hills, to safe, hot-slippered, weather-proof hearths, and wives called Mother, and old, fond, fleabag dogs, and the wireless babbling.

Young women from the offices, who smelt of scent and powder and wet pixie hoods and hair, scuttled, giggling, arm-in-arm, after hissing trams, and screeched as they splashed their stockings in the puddles rainbowed with oil between the slippery lines . . .

We walked towards the Marlborough, dodging umbrella spokes, smacked by our windy macs, stained by steaming lamplight, seeing the sodden blown scourings and street-wash of the town, papers, rags, dregs, rinds, fag-ends, balls of fur, flap, float, and cringe along the gutters, hearing the sneeze and rattle of the bony trams and a ship hoot like a fog-ditched owl in the bay, . . .

Dylan Thomas, THE FOLLOWERS

B Comment on the effect of the figurative language in the following extract.

Janice threw wide the closet door and almost screamed. Darkness and night and all the spaces between the stars looked out at her.

Long years ago two things had happened. Her sister had locked her, shrieking, in a closet. And, at a party, playing hide-and-seek, she had run through the kitchen and into a long dark hall. But it wasn't a hall. It was an unlit stair well, a swallowing blackness. She had run out upon empty air. She had pedalled her feet, screamed and fallen! Fallen in midnight blackness. Into the cellar. It took a long while, a heartbeat, to fall. And she had smothered in that closet a long, long time without daylight, without friends, no one to hear her screamings. Away from everything, locked in darkness. Falling in darkness. Shrieking!

The two memories.

Now, with the closet door wide, with darkness like a velvet shroud hung before her to be stroked by a trembling hand, with the darkness like a black panther breathing there, looking at her with unlit eyes, the two memories rushed out.

Ray Bradbury, THE WILDERNESS

C Find as many words as you can similar in meaning to each of the following. Say what kind of impression (favourable, neutral, unfavourable) each of your versions would convey to a reader.

loud

house

to sing

to eat

to look

D Write two accounts of a meal, one using words that create a favourable impression, and the other using words that create an unfavourable impression.

E How many different adjectives can you think of to describe a house, a child and the sea? How many different adverbs can you think of to describe walking, speaking and laughing?

F Write two short paragraphs, the first using active verbs and the second using passive verbs. Comment on the differences in effect between them.

G Write a short description in which figurative language plays an important part. It could be of a crowded street or an old castle or the sea-shore.

6◆*Things to Avoid*

Sometimes writers are lazy and put down the first words that come into their heads instead of thinking of fresh and interesting ways of saying what they want to say. Sometimes they are careless and express themselves badly. Here are some things you should avoid in your own writing.

Clichés

These are words and expressions that have been so overused that they no longer have any freshness or interest. Examples are 'in this day and age', 'when all's said and done', 'at the drop of a hat', 'to toss and turn', 'put your best foot forward'.

Vogue words

These are words and expressions which suddenly become fashionable and are used by everyone. Examples are 'brilliant', 'spin-off', 'a low profile', 'an on-going situation', 'an ego trip'.

Faded figurative language

This consists of metaphors and similes which are so overused that there is no originality left in them. For example: 'to feather your nest', 'to smell a rat', 'as red as a beetroot', 'as bold as brass', 'green with envy'.

Inevitable adjectives

Do not simply choose the first adjective that comes to mind as it is likely to be a cliché. Examples of inevitable adjectives are 'a crying shame', 'a general exodus', 'vital clues', 'a blushing bride', 'blissful ignorance'.

Solecisms

Solecisms are expressions that go against the generally accepted conventions of the grammar of Standard English. Examples are 'we was late', 'I couldn't of carried on', 'different than', 'I done it myself'. These should be avoided when writing standard English.

Ambiguity

Sometimes writing is not clearly expressed with the result that the meaning is not altogether certain. For example:

I wish there were more interesting films on television.

In this example, the meaning is ambiguous.

Tautology

This is the name given to the fault of saying the same thing twice. For example,

He left the room briefly for a short time.

(See also *Reading and Understanding*, Chapter 8, 'Stale Language'.)

A   Rewrite the following so as to eliminate any clichés.

1   This remarkable novel has struck a responsive chord in the hearts of thousands of readers. Its success is not likely to be eclipsed in our generation. It has rightly captured the imagination of an enormous public.

2   The buoyant tourist industry has made enormous strides in recent years. Millions of people are buying British in no uncertain terms. It just proves that when we put our minds to it, we can do it.

3   Arsenal fireball Ron Sellars is the sensational transfer target for League champions Everton. The double winners have made a new striker their No. 1 priority and Sellars has jumped to the head of the queue.

4   Movie giants Rank have put their foot down. They have banned big-name stars from appearing on Terry Wogan's TV chat show. Furious Hollywood moguls claim the Emerald Isle's master of blarney doesn't give the actors a fair chance to plug their latest films.

5   People who hide their light under a bushel are few and far between nowadays. Most people enjoy the limelight. They long for a bit of showbiz razzmatazz. They'll do anything for a taste of that glamorous world with its bubbling champagne and bright lights and cheering crowds.

B   How effective do you think the language is in the following extracts? Can you find ways of improving it?

1   Ibiza, smallest of the big three Balearic Islands, stands midway between the Spanish mainland and the North African coast. Bathed in dazzling sunlight, this easy-going island offers the full range of holidays choices. Peace and quiet in relaxing fishing village resorts, ideal for family beach holidays. Or the panache and glamour of the sophisticated spots with the jet-set image and reputation, such a favourite with the young. Whatever you choose you can be sure of sun-filled days in this glorious climate.

FLAIR SUMMER BROCHURE

2

Majorca, largest of the Balearic Islands, has long been the number one sunspot abroad for the British. And fully deserves the compliment too. To begin with, it boasts over 300 sunny days a year. Add to this a breathtakingly varied set of attractions. From the rugged charm of the mountainous north to the windmill dotted plains around Palma. From rocky coves to miles of sunswept sandy beaches. And the unsophisticated fishing village resorts are never more than an hour or two by road from the glitz and glamour of the Capital by night. Many contrasts. Infinite variety. Majorca offers holidays to suit all tastes, all pockets and all ages.

FLAIR SUMMER BROCHURE

C Write improved versions of the following sentences.

1 Only the loyal few among we Arsenal supporters were confident Arsenal would win.

2 Turning to the right the church appeared square and solid.

3 Everyone roared their heads off.

4 Between you and I there is something funny going on.

5 There were less people at the football match than usually attended.

6 What he said to you is different than what he said to me.

7 I can't do nothing about that.

8 All I want to do is lay down and go to sleep.

9 Do you know who you're talking to?

10 The reason why he couldn't reach the apple on the top branch of the tree was because he wasn't tall enough.

D   Rewrite the following sentences so that their meanings are clear and unambiguous.

    1   A patient had died in the chair of dental surgeon Moray Smith for the second time.

    2   Only gym shoes are to be worn inside the gym.

    3   This book can be recommended to many people who think they can write as well as beginners.

    4   The sudden gust of wind at the ceremony blew hats off, and copies of the vicar's speech and other rubbish were scattered over the churchyard.

    5   The cottage called Meadow Bank was knocked down for £50 000 by the auctioneer, Mr George Mason.

    6   Following the retirement of the headmaster, Mr Philip Newton, a thanksgiving service is to be held.

    7   She did not shout at the child because she was tired.

    8   I promise to return the form you sent me on Friday.

    9   Men like football more than women.

  10   I couldn't bring myself to reprimand the hard working man for the mess he had left.

E   Rewrite the following sentences eliminating any tautology.

    1   The ever rising number of unemployed is increasing all the time.

    2   Personally, I think they should bring back hanging.

    3   What I mean to say is, hanging people is wrong, after all, isn't it?

    4   His new discovery will, of course, revolutionise our present methods of making paper.

    5   In my opinion, I do not think the sole monopoly of supplying school uniforms to the school should be in the hands of Messrs Rawlinsons, the outfitters.

    6   These park gates are closed at 7.00 p.m. in the evening.

    7   The future outlook is grim for the joint partnership.

    8   I like this equally as well as the other.

    9   Fish abound in great numbers along the coast.

  10   He refused to help in any way, shape or form.

7◆Developing Ideas

Sometimes writers have difficulty in thinking up ideas and in developing ideas. Even experienced writers can suffer from what is known as writer's block when they feel stuck and unable to write a single word. When this happened to the actor Robert Shaw who also wrote a number of novels, he used to get up and read a few sentences from a book – any book. The purpose was not to steal someone else's ideas, but to immerse himself in words – and that usually set his own words flowing.

Here are some suggestions for getting ideas and developing ideas.

Thinking

Work away in your mind at the title or subject of your piece of writing. Think about different angles from which it could be approached. If it is a story, consider possible characters or settings or incidents. See if there is anything in your own experience which you could use or adapt. If it is an argument, consider whether there is a geographical or historical or political or religious or economic or social or moral angle you can explore. Consider how different people – children, pensioners, politicians, tourists, foreigners, farmers, conservationists, men, women – might respond.

Talking

Discussing a subject with other people – friends, teachers, family, neighbours – can suggest ideas. Their experience is different from your own, and they might have a different point of view which sparks off your own thinking. They might also be able to provide details and examples and arguments that you have not thought of.

Research

Reading a story by someone else on the subject might suggest how you could treat it yourself. It might help you to recall something in your own experience. Looking up a subject in a reference book might supply you with facts that you could use. Newspapers and television programmes might give you further information or a topical approach that you could develop.

Writing at length

Some people have difficulty in **expanding** their **thoughts** to a suitable length. The length of a piece of writing depends on a number of factors – the subject matter, the audience, the purpose, the degree of depth, for instance. But when it comes to an examination or to coursework, it is likely that you will be expected to write at least some pieces that are 500 or 600 words long.

If you have difficulty in filling out your thoughts to this kind of length, consider the following.

In stories and personal writing, ask yourself questions like these:

– Is there enough descriptive detail of people and places?

– Have incidents been fully and dramatically explored?

– Would another scene or incident be appropriate?

– Should another character be introduced so as to present another point of view?

– Have the thoughts and feelings of the characters been explored?

– Would a scene using dialogue help to dramatise the situation and make the attitudes of the characters clearer?

– Would figurative language make the situation or a character's feelings more vivid?

In an argumentative essay, ask yourself questions like these:

– Have both sides been fully explored (if that is required)?

– Have different angles been considered (for example, social, moral, historical, etc.)?

– Have the viewpoints of different people been considered (for example, children, men, women, etc.)?

– Are there examples and illustrations that could be used?

– Is there any personal experience or anecdote that could be used?

– Would an image or comparison make the argument clearer and more convincing?

– Is there any topical reference (about local events or what has appeared in newspapers or on television) that could be included?

A Write down any ideas that the following subjects suggest to you about how they might be treated.

1 The last rose of summer   4 A rolling stone

2 In the park   5 Nuclear energy.

3 Good intentions

B Discuss different kinds of approaches that might be possible for each of the following subjects.

1 Spare the rod   4 Friends and enemies

2 Under the earth   5 Far away and long ago.

3 The old folks at home

C   The following is a simple account of a childish prank. Rewrite it, expanding it to at least 500 words and making it more dramatic. Where appropriate, describe places and people, use dialogue, describe feelings, provide more conflict and contrast between the characters, build up the suspense.

> Tricia was the one who started it. She and I were mooching about not knowing what to do when she suggested we ring the bell of the big house on the corner and run away.
>
> Tricia did it first. I stood at the gate and watched and then ran like mad. Tricia came pelting after me. We hid behind the hedge of one of the houses across the lane and peeped round, but we couldn't see the door of the big house, and nobody came to the gate.
>
> Then it was my turn. I was terrified. I rang the bell, but this time, the door was jerked open straightaway, and there was a man there. We took off like a shot, and the man shouted after us.
>
> We ran to my house at the bottom of the lane. We thought we were safe. But then the man came and knocked at the door. He told Mum all about it. We had to write letters of apology and go and give them to the man at the big house.

D   Here are some views on school uniform. They could be fuller and more convincing. Using further arguments and examples, illustrations, personal experience, the views of parents and teachers, expand these ideas into an essay of at least 500 words.

> Who wants to wear school uniform? People say it's smarter, but I don't think so. Half my friends have grown out of their blazers and the sleeves are halfway up their arms, and nobody wears the tie properly done up.
>
> It's supposed to give you a sense of pride, showing you belong to a particular school. But I don't want people to know what school I go to.
>
> That's another thing. It's supposed to encourage you to behave yourself properly outside school. Because if you don't, people will know from your uniform what school you go to and complain. But wearing school uniform doesn't have any effect on the way some of our pupils behave.
>
> People say having school uniform prevents class distinctions. But my mum says school uniform is more expensive than other clothes, and why can't we wear jeans?
>
> School is supposed to help you develop your own standards and taste. But how can you do that when they just tell you what to wear?

8❖Planning and Structure

Some writers just sit down and put their words straight onto the page, but most writers have to think long about what they are going to write. They have to prepare it and plan it, draft it and redraft it.

If what you write simply rambles on, then it is unlikely to be effective. It needs to have a shape and a structure, and in order to ensure this, planning is likely to be necessary.

The first stage involves **thinking** about what you are going to write and **jotting down notes and ideas**. These may be descriptions of the main characters and the differences between them which lead to a conflict. Or details about a day at the seaside which you would then use in a description.

The next stage is to work out **the best way to present your material**. For instance, you might begin a story at the end and then show how events led up to that conclusion. You might balance the views for a particular argument with those against it. You might follow a chronological framework for a description of a day at the seaside, starting in the morning and going through to the evening.

Make a plan of what you are going to write, step by step. It need not be very elaborate or go into great detail. The idea is to make sure you know the direction you are going in once you actually start writing. For instance, a plan for a story might be like this:

A and B quarrel

B thinks over the quarrel and feels resentful

B talks to C who encourages B to get his own back on A

B tries to get A into trouble and fails

B ends up quarrelling with C.

For an argumentative essay, you might use a plan like this:

Introduction leading into the subject

Four arguments in favour

Four arguments against

Conclusion.

These outlines can then be filled out with details from the ideas you have already thought about, together with new ideas.

Write your story or essay following your plan – though there may be times when new ideas strike you and your plan may be modified. Make sure your language and tone are appropriate.

Read what you have written and consider it critically. Does it say what you wanted to say? Does it have a clearly defined shape and structure? How could it be improved?

Revise and **redraft** what you have written. This could involve things like rewriting sections, cutting and/or expanding, altering the structure, refining the language, reconstructing sentences, introducing new ideas and details.

(See also *Reading and Understanding*, Chapter 11, 'Structure and Development'.)

A   Examine the structure of the short story 'I Spy' (in Chapter 11). Reconstruct the plan the writer might have made before writing it.

B   Work out plans for each of the following pieces of writing:

1   A story about a child who gets lost

2   The advantages and disadvantages of rail travel

3   A personal account of an embarrassing or frustrating experience

4   Views on fashion

5   City lights.

C   Choose one of your plans for the above and develop it into a finished piece of writing. Revise and redraft it where necessary. Present all the various stages of your work.

D   Here are two versions of an extract from D.H. Lawrence's short story 'Odour of Chrysanthemums'. The first is a manuscript version, and the second is how it appeared in the published text. Examine and comment on the changes that have taken place and their effect.

MANUSCRIPT VERSION

Then they heard the girl calling shrilly upstairs:
"Mother—who is it?—who is it?—Mother!"
Elizabeth caught herself up, and going towards the stairs, she called:
"Go to sleep—it's nothing—go to sleep, and don't be silly"—then she went upstairs:
"What are you calling for? It's only your father, and he won't make any noise. Go to sleep now."
"I thought it was some men come!" wailed the child.
"They only came with your father—and you must go to sleep, he won't make any noise. He's asleep."
"Is he in bed?"
"Yes. And don't wake him. Go to sleep now."

"What time is it?"—the pitiful thin voice of the half comforted girl, and the plaintive question, were too much for the men downstairs. One by one they got their caps, and stepping over the body, they tiptoed out of the house, hearing the mother answer as they went:

"Ten o'clock!—There, go to sleep now." Her voice too was dreadful in its tenderness. They knew she kissed the children; and the little ones sank down again straight to sleep. So was the terror lifted off their hearts.

PUBLISHED TEXT

Then they heard the girl's voice upstairs calling shrilly: "Mother, mother—who is it? Mother, who is it?"

Elizabeth hurried to the foot of the stairs and opened the door:

"Go to sleep!" she commanded sharply. "What are you shouting about? Go to sleep at once—there's nothing—"

Then she began to mount the stairs. They could hear her on the boards, and on the plaster floor of the little bedroom. They could hear her distinctly:

"What's the matter now?—what's the matter with you, silly thing?"—her voice was much agitated, with an unreal gentleness.

"I thought it was some men come," said the plaintive voice of the child. "Has he come?"

"Yes, they've brought him. There's nothing to make a fuss about. Go to sleep now, like a good child."

They could hear her voice in the bedroom, they waited whilst she covered the children under the bedclothes.

"Is he drunk?" asked the girl, timidly, faintly.

"No! No—he's not! He—he's asleep."

"Is he asleep downstairs?"

"Yes—and don't make a noise."

There was silence for a moment, then the men heard the frightened child again:

"What's that noise?"

"It's nothing, I tell you, what are you bothering for?"

The noise was the grandmother moaning. She was oblivious of everything, sitting on her chair rocking and moaning. The manager put his hand on her arm and bade her "Sh-sh!!"

The old woman opened her eyes and looked at him. She was shocked by this interruption, and seemed to wonder.

"What time is it?"—the plaintive thin voice of the child, sinking back unhappily into sleep, asked this last question.

"Ten o'clock," answered the mother more softly. Then she must have bent down and kissed the children.

Matthews beckoned to the men to come away. They put on their caps and took up the stretcher. Stepping over the body, they tiptoed out of the house. None of them spoke till they were far from the wakeful children.

D.H. Lawrence, 'Odour of Chrysanthemums'
(from manuscript and published versions)

9◆*Opening and Ending*

How you open and how you end a piece of writing are important. Your opening should catch your readers' attention so that they want to read on. Your ending should leave your readers feeling satisfied that the time spent in reading your piece has been worthwhile.

George Orwell, for instance, opens his novel *1984* with this sentence:

> It was a bright cold day in April, and the clocks were striking thirteen.

William Makepeace Thackeray ends a chapter in *Vanity Fair* describing the Battle of Waterloo like this:

> No more firing was heard at Brussels – the pursuit rolled miles away.
> Darkness came down on the field and city: and Amelia was praying for
> George, who was lying on his face, dead, with a bullet through his heart.

How effective do you think these examples are?

Openings

In **a story**, the opening might:

- Establish a character or a setting or an action

- Make a general statement that the story is going to illustrate

- Be a question or a piece of dialogue.

Whatever it is, it must capture the readers' interest and have a bearing on what the story is about.

In **an article**, **a description** or **an argumentative essay**, the opening might be:

- A general or controversial statement

- A quotation or a topical reference

- A witty, neatly-balanced sentence

- A question

- Figures or statistics

- A striking image or an example

- A joke or an anecdote.

It can be effective to open with something which at first sight might not appear to have much relevance to the main subject of the writing – although later it will be clear that it is relevant. In other words, you could approach the subject at a tangent.

Endings

A story could end:

- On a dramatic note

- On a thoughtful comment

- With a character reflecting on the experience

- With an action that brings the story full circle

- With an ironic comment that reveals the events in a different light.

Your ending should have a sense of inevitability and completeness about it. It should help readers to look back at the whole experience of the story, see how it has been shaped, and feel that the events have been given a satisfying unity.

An article, **a description** or **an argumentative essay** could end:

- With a strong final statement that sums up the case

- With a quotation or a topical reference

- With a question

- With an illustrative joke or anecdote

- With a witty, neatly balanced sentence

- With an example taken from personal experience

- With a striking image.

If you are summing up, do not repeat what you have already said. Try to think of a different angle which leaves the reader with something new but relevant to think about.

A Look at the following openings to short stories. How effective are they, as far as you can tell? What do you think each story might be about, judging from the opening?

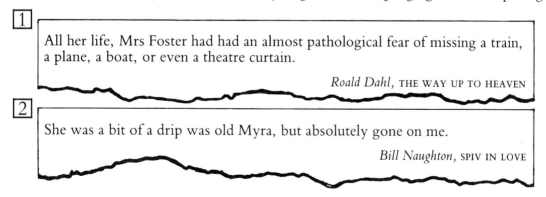

1

> All her life, Mrs Foster had had an almost pathological fear of missing a train, a plane, a boat, or even a theatre curtain.
>
> *Roald Dahl,* THE WAY UP TO HEAVEN

2

> She was a bit of a drip was old Myra, but absolutely gone on me.
>
> *Bill Naughton,* SPIV IN LOVE

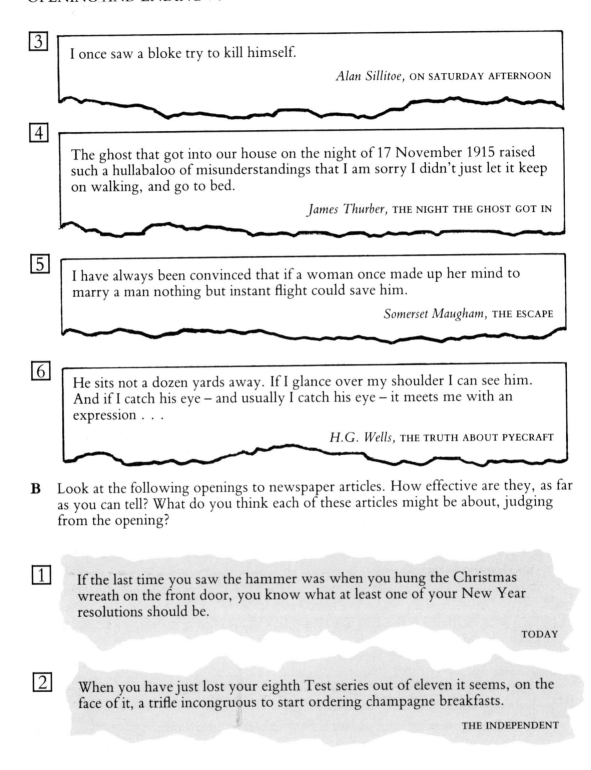

3 I once saw a bloke try to kill himself.

Alan Sillitoe, ON SATURDAY AFTERNOON

4 The ghost that got into our house on the night of 17 November 1915 raised such a hullabaloo of misunderstandings that I am sorry I didn't just let it keep on walking, and go to bed.

James Thurber, THE NIGHT THE GHOST GOT IN

5 I have always been convinced that if a woman once made up her mind to marry a man nothing but instant flight could save him.

Somerset Maugham, THE ESCAPE

6 He sits not a dozen yards away. If I glance over my shoulder I can see him. And if I catch his eye – and usually I catch his eye – it meets me with an expression . . .

H.G. Wells, THE TRUTH ABOUT PYECRAFT

B Look at the following openings to newspaper articles. How effective are they, as far as you can tell? What do you think each of these articles might be about, judging from the opening?

1 If the last time you saw the hammer was when you hung the Christmas wreath on the front door, you know what at least one of your New Year resolutions should be.

TODAY

2 When you have just lost your eighth Test series out of eleven it seems, on the face of it, a trifle incongruous to start ordering champagne breakfasts.

THE INDEPENDENT

3

Against the suntanned bodies sprawled along the miles of golden Acapulco sands, Phil Collins's white body stood out like a lone snow-flake at Christmas.

DAILY EXPRESS

4

Arnold Schwarzenegger is far easier to watch than to spell.

DAILY MAIL

5

The flames licked hungrily around our smarting, sooty eyes as we crouched together in the dark blustery night over a gypsy campfire.

DAILY MIRROR

6

Jeffrey Archer needs no introduction, and it is unlikely his books will ever qualify for one.

THE GUARDIAN

C   Look at the following endings to short stories. How effective are they, as far as you can tell? What do you think each of these stories might be about, judging from the ending?

1

He said, 'I'm sorry. I can't help it, Mr Thomas. There's nothing personal, but you've got to admit it's funny.'

Graham Greene, THE DESTRUCTORS

2

She put him down and he began to scrape out the pudding-basin, certain at least of one thing, that grown-ups were mad and silly and he hated them all, all, *all.*

John Wain, A MESSAGE FROM THE PIG-MAN

3

I had never seen her smile before, but she was smiling now.

James Thurber, THE DEPARTURE OF EMMA INCH

4

She gave me such a clout, I thought my head was going to fall off. My mum never believes me – even when I'm telling the truth.

George Layton, THE FIB

5

And thus it came to pass that in the dusk of a November evening the Russian boy, murmuring a few of the prayers of his Church for luck, gave hasty but decent burial to a large polecat under the lilac trees at Hoopington.

Saki, THE BAG

6

But Lilian was not listening. She was thinking of the stranger from Lagos and wishing she had been braver.

Cyprian Ekwensi, A STRANGER FROM LAGOS

D Look at the following endings to newspaper articles. How effective are they, as far as you can tell? What do you think each of these articles might be about, judging from the ending?

1

No longer is there, as one former manager was mixed-metaphorically moved to say: 'A rat in the camp trying to throw a spanner in the works'.

THE GUARDIAN

2

'There is no use teaching them one thing in school and their parents practising another at home.'

THE SUN

3

So it is unlikely the full toll will ever be known about the worst maritime disaster since the *Titanic*.

DAILY EXPRESS

4

Not for nothing is St Moritz's unofficial motto: 'If you want it – and can pay for it – you can have it.'

DAILY MAIL

5

A spokesman said: 'Obviously Millwall are known for a small element who cause trouble, but we will not be tarring every fan with the same brush.'

DAILY MIRROR

6

They have much in common with military commanders in the heat of battle, with their men sometimes leaving the field on stretchers when this sport reaches its often violent climax.

THE GUARDIAN

E Find further examples of openings and endings of short stories and articles which you consider effective. Justify your choice.

F Suggest openings and endings that might be effective for each of the following:

1 A report on facilities for pensioners in your area

2 A story about someone losing a race or a competition

3 A personal account of a part-time job

4 A description of a busy shopping centre

5 An essay arguing against school uniform.

10◆Variety of Writing

Writing can take many forms, but broadly it can be divided into three different types – expressive writing, persuasive writing and informative writing.

Expressive writing

This is writing that appeals to the intellect, the feelings and the imagination – for example, fiction, poetry.

Persuasive writing

This is writing that attempts to win the reader over to a particular point of view – for example, editorials, political pamphlets.

Informative writing

This is writing that provides information – for example, a public health leaflet, a recipe.

Type of writing and intention

Identifying the category to which a piece of writing belongs can help you to determine the intention behind the writing. Having a clear idea of the category to which a piece of your own writing belongs can help you to adopt the right language and tone for the audience you are addressing. For instance, if the intention is to inform, you might use simpler language and shorter, more direct sentences.

Note that it is possible for a piece of writing to belong to more than one category, that is, to have more than one intention behind it. For instance, it can be claimed that much fiction is didactic (that is, it is trying to teach the reader something – about human relationships or about a moral situation). Fiction of this kind can therefore be regarded as both expressive and persuasive (or even informative).

You will be expected to provide writing of various types in your coursework. Your teacher will tell you what the particular requirements are for the syllabus you are following.

A Examine the following pieces of writing. Say what kind of writing each is (that is, expressive, persuasive, informative). Remember that some writing may belong to more than one category. Say also to what extent the kind of writing each is affects the language and tone used.

1

In the first place, fashion in the Kings Road was almost entirely female. Mary Quant had opened Bazaar in 1955 and, on her success, rivals sprang up in groups. The street became famous, and filled with frivolities of every kind, and tourists visited it from all around the world just to sample its fol-de-rol treats, and all this time, there was only one men's shop that counted – John Michael. Clearly, there was a gap to be filled and, from the mid-sixties on, Carnaby Street began to move in.

Nik Cohn, TODAY THERE ARE NO GENTLEMEN

2 Sometimes the factory was a refuge from the world. The noise that battered you on every side could also protect you. Normal talk was impossible. Communication needed a tremendous effort and some ingenuity. You had to pitch your voice high, condense your message to the barest minimum, supplement shouted words with gestures.

Ralph Glasser, GROWING UP IN THE GORBALS

3

The woman put her sad moon-face in at the window of the car. 'You be good,' she said. 'You hear me? You little ones, mind what Dicey tells you. You hear?'
    'Yes, Momma,' they said.
    'That's all right then.' She slung her purse over her shoulder and walked away, her stride made uneven by broken sandal thongs, thin elbows shoving through holes in the oversized sweater, her jeans faded and baggy.

Cynthia Voigt, HOMECOMING

4

The conservationists are in a tizz this week because the Government is suggesting that the planning controls over some advertising signs might be relaxed. The curious thing about England today is how few of these signs there are, by comparison with the past. Edwardian photographs show towns dense with hoardings. The dwindling of their numbers hasn't improved us culturally, intellectually, psychologically. A few more signs won't do us any harm.

Paul Barker, THE SUNDAY TELEGRAPH

5

Gregory Underwood was happy.

It wasn't the fulfilled man's quiet feeling that all is well with the world. It wasn't the sudden benediction granted by a moment of great triumph or unexpected good news. It was sudden, yes, unexpected – certainly – but it came from nowhere. A surge from the subconscious, a brilliance of heart and brain. He glowed.

It was happening to him quite a lot these days.

His father put it down to hormones. Not that Mr Underwood – a quiet, gingery man who taught nervous housewives to drive – had any special insight into his son's mental condition.

Gerald Cole, GREGORY'S GIRL

B You may be asked to provide some of the following in your coursework. Say what kind of writing each is likely to be. Say also how the type of writing a particular piece belongs to may affect the language and tone you use.

personal writing

a story

an argumentative essay

an advertisement

a newspaper report

a description

a character sketch

writing in response to reading

an explanation, directions or instructions

a report

a poem

a play

a letter

writing about a picture

C Examine the writing in your coursework. Decide what kind of writing each piece is. See whether your writing covers the requirements for coursework set by the syllabus you are following.

Part Two

Looking at Particular Aspects of Writing

11 ◆ A Story

When planning and writing a story, you need to consider the following.

Plot

Make sure the events of your story are believable – unless you are deliberately being fantastic. Do not try to cover too many events. Keep to something simple (for example, a meeting, a quarrel, a special occasion) and describe it in depth.

Characters

Make sure your characters are convincing. Make sure they have names and attitudes and personalities that distinguish one from another so that the reader can identify them (for example, different characters might be resentful, narrow-minded or easy-going). Show them in dialogue and action that are consistent with their personalities and which demonstrate their attitudes.

Setting

Make sure your setting is convincing by using descriptive details and references. Your setting can be quite ordinary (for example, someone's home, school, a country road). Make sure your setting is relevant to the action and the characters.

Structure

Make sure your story has a shape. The events of the story should have a unity about them so that the reader is able to look back at the story as a whole and see it as a complete and satisfying experience.

Point of view

Decide from whose point of view the events of the story are being seen. Is it you – the author – describing the events in an objective way? Are the events being seen through the eyes of a particular character? The point of view you decide on will affect the language and tone you use.

Purpose

Most stories have a purpose behind them – that is, a reason why the writer thinks it worthwhile to take the trouble to write it. The purpose may be simply to entertain, or it may be to put across an issue in fictional form, or it may be to say something about human nature or about the relationships between people. Think about the purpose of your own story. What do you want the reader to learn from it? Why should the reader bother to read it?

All these aspects are interrelated. Actions (that is, the plot) can arise out of characters, the setting can affect how characters behave, and so on. Thinking about one can help you to work out the others. For instance, if you are writing about a timid character, how would he or she react in a strange town?

You can often get your imagination working on a story by thinking about people or places you know or about things that have happened to you. The writer Brian Glanville has said, 'A short story may begin – the grit in the oyster – with an incident, an anecdote, a person, an idea.'

(See also Chapter 7, 'Developing Ideas', Chapter 8, 'Planning and Structure', and Chapter 9, 'Opening and Ending'.)

A Read the following story.

I Spy

Charlie Stowe waited until he heard his mother snore before he got out of bed. Even then he moved with caution and tiptoed to the window. The front of the house was irregular, so that it was possible to see a light burning in his mother's room. But now all the windows were dark. A searchlight passed across the sky, lighting the banks of cloud and probing the dark deep spaces between, seeking enemy airships. The wind blew from the sea, and Charlie Stowe could hear behind his mother's snores the beating of the waves. A draught through the cracks in the window-frame stirred his nightshirt. Charlie Stowe was frightened.

But the thought of the tobacconist's shop which his father kept down a dozen wooden stairs drew him on. He was twelve years old, and already boys at the County School mocked him because he had never smoked a cigarette. The packets were piled twelve deep below, Gold Flake and Players, De Reszke, Abdulla, Woodbines, and the little shop lay under a thin haze of stale smoke which would completely disguise his crime. That it was a crime to steal some of his father's stock Charlie Stowe had no doubt, but he did not love his father; his father was unreal to him, a wraith, pale, thin, indefinite, who noticed him only spasmodically and left even punishment to his mother. For his mother he felt a passionate demonstrative love; her large boisterous presence and her noisy charity filled the world for him; from her speech he judged her the friend of everyone, from the rector's wife to the 'dear Queen', except the 'Huns', the monsters who lurked in Zeppelins in the clouds. But his father's affection and dislike were as indefinite as his movements. Tonight he had said he would be in Norwich, and yet you never knew. Charlie Stowe had no sense of safety as he crept down the wooden stairs. When they creaked he clenched his fingers on the collar of his nightshirt.

At the bottom of the stairs he came out quite suddenly into the little shop. It was too dark to see his way, and he did not dare touch the switch. For half a minute he sat in despair on the bottom step with his chin cupped in his hands. Then the regular movement of the searchlight was reflected through an upper window and the boy had time to fix in memory the pile of cigarettes, the counter, and the small hole under it. The footsteps of a policeman on the pavement made him grab the first packet to his hand and dive for the hole. A light shone along the floor and a hand tried the door, then the footsteps passed on, and Charlie cowered in the darkness.

At last he got his courage back by telling himself in his curiously adult way that if he were caught now there was nothing to be done about it, and he might as well have his smoke. He put a cigarette in his mouth and then remembered that he had no matches. For a while he dared not move. Three times the searchlight lit the shop, while he muttered taunts and encouragements. 'May as well be hung for a sheep', 'Cowardy, cowardy custard,' grown-up and childish exhortations oddly mixed.

But as he moved he heard footfalls in the street, the sound of several men walking rapidly. Charlie Stowe was old enough to feel surprise that anybody was about. The footsteps came nearer, stopped; a key was turned in the shop door, a voice said: 'Let him in,' and then he heard his father, 'If you wouldn't mind being quiet, gentlemen. I don't want to wake up the family.' There was a note unfamiliar to Charlie in the undecided voice. A torch flashed and the electric globe burst into blue light. The boy held his breath; he wondered whether his father would hear his heart beating, and he clutched his nightshirt tightly and prayed, 'O God, don't let me be caught.' Through a crack in the counter he could see his father where he stood, one hand held to his high stiff collar, between two men in bowler hats and belted mackintoshes. They were strangers.

'Have a cigarette,' his father said in a voice dry as a biscuit. One of the men shook his head. 'It wouldn't do, not when we are on duty. Thank you all the same.' He spoke gently, but without kindness: Charlie Stowe thought his father must be ill.

'Mind if I put a few in my pocket?' Mr Stowe asked, and when the man nodded he lifted a pile of Gold Flake and Players from a shelf and caressed the packets with the tips of his fingers.

'Well,' he said, 'there's nothing to be done about it, and I may as well have my smokes.' For a moment Charlie Stowe feared discovery, his father stared round the shop so thoroughly; he might have been seeing it for the first time. 'It's a good little business,' he said, 'for those that like it. The wife will sell out, I suppose. Else the neighbours'll be wrecking it. Well, you want to be off. A stitch in time. I'll get my coat.'

'One of us'll come with you, if you don't mind,' said the stranger gently.

'You needn't trouble. It's on the peg here. There, I'm all ready.'

The other man said in an embarrassed way, 'Don't you want to speak to your wife?' The thin voice was decided, 'Not me. Never do today what you can put off till tomorrow. She'll have her chance later, won't she?'

'Yes, yes,' one of the strangers said and he became very cheerful and encouraging. 'Don't you worry too much. While there's life . . .' and suddenly his father tried to laugh.

When the door had closed Charlie Stowe tiptoed upstairs and got into bed. He wondered why his father had left the house again so late at night and who the strangers were. Surprise and awe kept him for a little while awake. It was as if a familiar photograph had stepped from the frame to reproach him with neglect. He remembered how his father had held tight to his collar and fortified himself with proverbs, and he thought for the first time that, while his mother was boisterous and kindly, his father was very like himself, doing things in the dark which frightened him. It would have pleased him to go down to his father and tell him that he loved him, but he could hear through the window the quick steps going away. He was alone in the house with his mother, and he fell asleep.

Graham Greene, COLLECTED STORIES

1   Briefly summarise the plot. Do you find it believable?

2   Describe the character of Charlie. How does the writer make him convincing? Are his feelings at the end of the story different from what they were at the beginning?

3   Describe Charlie's parents. How are they contrasted? In what ways is Charlie like his father?

4   Describe the setting and the time in which the story is set. What details does the writer use to make them convincing? How are they related to the events of the story?

5   Comment on the structure and shape of the story. Do you find it satisfying and complete in itself?

6   From whose point of view are the events seen? Why do you think the writer chose this point of view, and what effect does it have on the story?

7   What do you think the writer's purpose was in writing this story?

B   Write a story about one of the following:

1   No way out

2   A story about rivalry and jealousy between two brothers or two sisters

3   A story about a family disaster – this could be treated in a comic or a serious way

4   The new teacher

5   A story written from the point of view of a pensioner, or a ten-year-old child, or an immigrant, or a bully.

12◆Personal Writing

In personal writing, you are writing about yourself. Basically, there are two types of personal writing. In the first, you write about your own experiences and about incidents that happened to you or at which you were present. In the second, you give your feelings and thoughts about a subject.

Describing your experiences

When describing your experiences, you have to bear in mind the same kind of aspects that you would when writing a story. The plot, the characters, the setting and the structure are all important, even though you are basing them on what actually happened. You have to use the same kind of skills as you would in a story, and you have to give your experience a shape.

Obviously, in personal writing, the point of view is fixed. Everything has to be seen through your eyes, and you have to make clear your own reactions and reflections. This will influence the kind of language and tone you use.

You do not necessarily have to tell it exactly as it happened. You can invent details and dialogue. You can adapt events and characters. But you have to convince the reader that what you describe could have happened.

Giving your thoughts or feelings about a subject

When giving your thoughts or feelings about a subject, you could consider the following aspects:

- Your own experience of the subject

- How you first reacted to it

- Whether your feelings have changed in any way

- How you think other people react to it

- Specific examples to illustrate your response

- Points for and against the subject.

Again, things have to be seen essentially from your own point of view, and you have to ensure that what you write is planned and has a shape.

A Read this passage.

I was the last to arrive and the woman in charge, not my form teacher, frowned at her watch.

'You're late, we'll be starting in exactly two minutes. You're Valerie Avery, aren't you?'

How strange my name sounded. Perhaps it wasn't my name after all, perhaps I wasn't me but somebody else. What a queer name, Valerie Avery. I nodded and felt my mouth go parched.

'You'll sit at the back, and be quick.'

I sat down and put my lucky charms on the desk, kissing each one in turn—a feather I had found on the pavement a week ago, a little brass horse-shoe Mum had given me and Gran's gold sovereign.

'You have one hour starting from now,' came the voice, detached and hollow, like a station announcer.

The English composition wasn't too difficult. I liked writing stories, but the trouble was I got carried away. I was writing on the subject 'Shopping', and it was all about Mum and I going to the West End to buy Christmas presents, but on the bus I saw lots of exciting things, an accident, a fire, a robbery, then we just reached Oxford Circus when Mum found she'd lost her purse. We hadn't even started shopping when a hand snatched my paper away. I was in the middle of a word. I hadn't heard her say we had five minutes to go, and we were to make sure our names were on our papers. I was sure I hadn't done this and hadn't checked full-stops or commas, or capital letters. I was certain I hadn't done a thing right, but it was too late to worry about that, for now came the arithmetic paper. This I was dreading, yet it turned out much better than I expected. My gold sovereign was doing its work. I raced through the paper, I could do every one. I had finished all the sums, and checked them over, and there was still half an hour to go, so I sat back watching the rest tearing their hair and picking their noses. Then I studied the ears of those around me. I hadn't noticed till then what peculiar-looking things they were. They were all different, some big and flappy, elephant's ears, some small like sea shells, some like rashers of bacon stuck upside down on the sides of the head, some red, some pink, some blue. And the boy in front was making his ears wriggle. I tried to do the same, when I saw the woman walking towards me. 'Perhaps she thinks I'm cheating. She's got it in for me, the old faggot, perhaps she's jealous of my curls,' and I fondled one. But she bent over the girl sitting next to me who was snivelling. The woman whispered something, the girl sniffed back, the woman looked at her paper, pointed to something on it, the girl picked up her pen and wrote.

'Blimmin' cheek,' I thought. 'Still, Mum says cheats never prosper. Anyway, I've finished, so what do I care.'

The papers were collected in and I shivered with excitement. I knew I had done well. I would pass for a grammar school. I might even go to the same school as Janey Ascot. That'd show 'em. Wouldn't Mum be pleased. I kissed my gold sovereign. 'Thanks, Goldie.'

I skipped home, I was so happy, with two girls in my class, Fatty and Goofy.

'Easy, wasn't it?' I grinned.

'I don't think so,' Goofy's fangs bit through her bottom lip, 'especially the arithmetic.'

'I thought it was awful,' agreed Fatty, panting and flushing.

'How come?' I asked. 'If I could do it, surely you could.'

'But what about that last one, Val?' asked Fatty, her beady eyes protruding in a mass of pulp.

I stopped skipping. 'That was dead simple. Just a decimal. All you had to do was to put the dot in. Couldn't you do that?'

'That was all right,' said Fatty, gasping for breath, and turning purple. 'I meant the last one, about the stairs. How did you do that?'

'About the stairs?' I stopped walking. 'There wasn't one about stairs. There was nothing about stairs on my paper, was there on yours, Goof?'

'Yea, but I couldn't do it. I just looked at it and gave up.'

'But I don't know what you're talking about,' I shouted. 'What stairs?'

'Ooh, Val,' Fatty's eyes came out on stalks and one of her purple chins wobbled, 'don't say you didn't see it. It was the last one, on the back of the paper. Don't say you didn't turn over. Mrs. Harris said we must be sure to have a go at all of them and to make sure to turn over the paper, because the last one carries the most marks, and you get marks just for trying. Ooh, Val.'

My blood turned to water. I crushed the feather in my hands and ran.

'Hey, wait, Val,' the girls called. 'What's got into her?'

I ran across the road without looking and a car hooted.

'Watch what you're doing, you silly little fool, I nearly ran you over.'

It didn't matter. I wish he had. I had done it all wrong. I wouldn't pass.

Valerie Avery, LONDON MORNING

1   Briefly summarise what this passage is about.

2   What impression do you get of the writer and her attitudes and feelings?

3   Describe the other main characters. How convincing do you find them?

4   How does the writer convince you that this experience actually happened to her? Refer to details, incidents, feelings, dialogue.

5   Comment on the language and tone. Are they appropriate?

6   How effective do you think the opening and ending are?

7   Has the writer given her experience a shape?

B   Choose one of the following to write about.

1   I wish I hadn't.

2   Write about an incident from your past when you felt afraid or anxious or jealous or spiteful.

3   Write about a day that you were particularly looking forward to. Your expectations might have been fulfilled or disappointed.

4   Me and my friends *or* Me and my enemies.

5   Moving house *or* Changing schools.

C   Read the following piece, written when the author was fourteen.

History can be the most fascinating and also the most boring of all school 'subjects'. Four years ago, in the primary school, we crouched spell-bound as the snake's prey before the glittering eyes of the Roman gladiator who clashed, smeared in dust, sweat and blackened blood, round the arena. One year later, tall flashing knights knelt in proud obeisance to queens with grave eyes and jewelled robes. The threadbare, red-and-white banners crumpled in salute – to ourselves. Then, a scrunch of pebbles, a sucking of wavelets, a fanfare of golden trumpets, and grim William stood, shedding an aura of power and determination on Hastings' sandy dunes. A red swirl of events followed, until Drake's towering, creamy sails billowed to the firmament before a wild wind. But the sails fluttered and died, and the wind skirled over the edge of the world into black nothingness. It has never come back.

At the end of the third year I drew a line under 'History' in a printed form. I have since been labouring my way through a grey, mechanical tangle of drudgery, or 'British Social and Economic History, 1700 ——'. Actually, I enjoyed, relatively speaking, the two separate weeks on agriculture, as some groping feeler for the lost, pulsing freshness of life. The remaining fourth-year history (four periods a week, on, on, on) was engulfed under a jarring flood of facts, machines, names and dates. I now know by heart a long list of inventions in the eighteenth-century textile industry: John Kay, Flying Shuttle, 1733 . . . spinning machine with rollers, 1738 — it didn't work anyway; just how many tons of coal were produced at the most unlikely dates thoughout the two centuries, the physical mechanisms of Watt's steam engine, Bramah's patent water-closet and Nasmyth's steam hammer, as well as a host of other fragments. Shattered and flung about like the splinters of a broken jam-jar, how can all this superficial knowledge be gathered into the swelling, fluctuating flow of life which must have been there?

If I could reform my school I should do it on the principle of education through each pupil's own imagination. . . . It seems to me that it is the bored, fidgety pupils who cause the hold-ups (I speak from the same level). If everyone is kept intelligently amused, eagerness to carry on discovering history will surely follow. Interest should be maintained through films, group projects and discussions, not lectures. Pupils should be exhorted to imagine, imagine themselves there in the dirty mills or lofty House of Lords, imagine people talking, making decisions through lengthy arguments or sudden whims. Questions: 'What sort of *man* was Napoleon?' 'Do you think personal character had any influence on these political decisions?' should be posed, sometimes for class discussion, sometimes for homework, which could include projects and research with a few essays. . . .

I awake to a sickening thud each Monday morning — double History, eighty minutes of the toneless drone of the master's voice and the pendulum swing of his leg over the desk.

Judith, in Edward Blishen (ed.),
THE SCHOOL THAT I'D LIKE

1   Sum up briefly the point the writer is making.

2   Justify the view that this is a piece of **personal** writing.

3   How important is the use of contrast?

4   Does this piece of writing have a shape? Justify your view.

5   How similar is your own experience? Do you agree with the view presented here?

D   Choose one of the following to write about.

1   My hopes for the future

2   Choose a subject that fascinates you (for example, motorbikes, ice-skating, pets) and say why

3   Give your thoughts on racial prejudice

4   Sundays

5   The world of the teenager.

13◆*People*

In a story and in personal writing, you may have to describe or encapsulate a character in a short phrase or a sentence because you do not have many words at your disposal. You need to fix on specific details which help the reader to identify and visualise the character. You could:

- Describe physical details, posture or movement, dress, individual mannerisms

- Describe or indicate particular attitudes

- Give important points about background or past history

- Show the character through the eyes of other characters

- Use speech that is typical of the character

- Use figurative language to create a striking impression.

You can use all these methods too when writing a **character sketch** – that is, a piece of writing whose main purpose is to tell the reader about a particular character. Alternatively, you could pretend to be the character and allow the character to be revealed through his or her own words, as it were. This is a form of role-playing. By allowing the character to let his or her thoughts flow in what is known as stream of consciousness, or in reaction to a situation, you can show the kind of person the character is.

A Describe the methods used in the following extracts from short stories to describe the characters. How effective do you think each is in enabling the reader to gain an impression of the character?

1 On this night she was the stranger. A little Welsh girl, with a nice singy voice.

Bill Naughton, THE LITTLE WELSH GIRL

2 Hunched over the driver's wheel sat Kelly, the owner, a rock of a man with a huge head and broken fingernails.

Brian Friel, THE POTATO GATHERERS

3   John Gillan was a thickset man, wearing a raincoat that had been washed to a whitish colour and reached from his throat to the insteps of his black heavy boots.

Liam O'Flaherty, A POT OF GOLD

4   My mother didn't want me to go near the Concession stores because they smelled, and were dirty, and the natives spat tuberculosis germs into the dust. She said it was no place for little girls.

Nadine Gordimer, THE DEFEATED

5   His mates at the factory said Christie was only eleven-pence-ha'penny in the shilling, and had been ever since the war; but like the management, they tolerated him, because he was able-bodied and harmless, and for most of the time as near normal as hardly mattered.

Stan Barstow, THE SEARCH FOR TOMMY FLYNN

6   'I know of only one place hotter than this,' said Ahmed the Turk, alleged housebreaker, assaulter and stabber. He smiled, flashing his teeth the colour of ripe corn in his dark handsome face.

Alex la Guma, TATTOO MARKS AND NAILS

7   At the age of 17 Roger Merrit was a tall blond fellow with a high-pitched voice and a gangling stride that left his torso hanging just a little behind his legs when he walked.

Dan Jacobson, THE GAME

8   He was like the donkey he had tied in the front of his yard, grey and old and silent except when it brayed loudly.

V. S. Naipaul, GEORGE AND THE PINK HOUSE

9   Theodoric Valer had been brought up, from infancy to the confines of middle age, by a fond mother whose chief solicitude had been to keep him screened from what she called the coarser realities of life.

Saki, THE MOUSE

> | 10 |
>
> Miss Taylor had legs like bath loofahs stuffed into long, hairy grey socks, that were held up by tourniquets of narrow elastic.
>
> *Jan Mark,* THE CHOICE IS YOURS

B Write ten sentences, each of which pinpoints a character in an interesting way.

C 1 What effects are the writers trying to achieve in each of the following similes describing the voice of a character? How successful are they?

(a) His voice took on the quality of a cat snagging brushed nylon.
Douglas Adams

(b) His voice thickened as though blood were being stirred into it.
Anthony Burgess

(c) . . . as toneless as a police radio.
Raymond Chandler

(d) . . . husky, like an overworked rooster trying to croon.
Raymond Chandler

(e) . . . that could have been used for paint remover.
Raymond Chandler

(f) . . . that could have been used to defrost a refrigerator.
Rex Stout

(g) . . . that would have frozen an Eskimo.
P.G. Wodehouse

(h) . . . pursued him in anger, like that of a kennelled dog cheated of a walk.
Anthony Burgess

(i) . . . trickled like honey on biscuits.
Douglas Adams

(j) . . . like a concertina that has been left out in the rain.
Max Beerbohm

2 Find or invent similes to describe the following:

a smile

hair

a face

eyes

teeth.

D Compare the following passages describing people and the methods the writers use.

1

Perhaps one of the most weird and fascinating characters I met during my travels was the Rose-Beetle Man. He had a fairytale air about him that was impossible to resist, and I used to look forward eagerly to my infrequent meetings with him. I first saw him on a high, lonely road leading to one of the remote mountain villages. I could hear him long before I could see him, for he was playing a rippling tune on a shepherd's pipe, breaking off now and then to sing a few words in a curious, nasal voice. As he rounded the corner both Roger and I stopped and stared at him in amazement.

He had a sharp, fox-like face with large, slanting eyes of such a dark brown that they appeared black. They had a weird, vacant look about them, and a sort of bloom such as one finds on a plum, a pearly covering almost like a cataract. He was short and slight, with a thinness about his wrists and neck that argued a lack of food. His dress was fantastic, and on his head was a shapeless hat with a very wide, floppy brim. It had once been bottle-green, but was now speckled and smeared with dust, wine-stains, and cigarette burns. In the band were stuck a fluttering forest of feathers: cock-feathers, hoopoe-feathers, owl-feathers, the wing of a kingfisher, the claw of a hawk, and a large dirty white feather that may have come from a swan. His shirt was worn and frayed, grey with sweat, and round the neck dangled an enormous cravat of the most startling blue satin. His coat was dark and shapeless, with patches of different hues here and there; on the sleeve a bit of white cloth with a design of rosebuds; on the shoulder a triangular patch of wine-red and white spots. The pockets of this garment bulged, the contents almost spilling out: combs, balloons, little highly coloured pictures of the saints, olive-wood carvings of snakes, camels, dogs and horses, cheap mirrors, a riot of handkerchiefs, and long twisted rolls of bread decorated with seeds. His trousers, patched like his coat, dropped over a pair of scarlet *charouhias*, leather shoes with upturned toes decorated with a large black-and-white pompon. This extraordinary character carried on his back bamboo cages full of pigeons and young chickens, several mysterious sacks, and a large bunch of fresh green leeks. With one hand he held his pipe to his mouth, and in the other a number of lengths of cotton, to each of which was tied an almond-size rose-beetle, glittering golden green in the sun, all of them flying round his hat with desperate, deep buzzings, trying to escape from the thread tied firmly round their waists. Occasionally, tired of circling round and round without success, one of the beetles would settle for a moment on his hat before launching itself off once more on its endless merry-go-round.

Gerald Durrell, MY FAMILY AND OTHER ANIMALS

2

The door banged. She took her brushes and cloths into the bedroom. But when she began to make the bed, smoothing, tucking, patting, the thought of little Lennie was unbearable. Why did he have to suffer so? That's what she couldn't understand. Why should a little angel child have to ask for his breath and fight for it? There was no sense in making a child suffer like that.

. . . From Lennie's little box of a chest there came a sound as though something was boiling. There was a great lump of something bubbling in his chest that he couldn't get rid of. When he coughed, the sweat sprang out on his head: his eyes bulged, his hands waved, and the great lump bubbled as a potato knocks in a saucepan. But what was more awful than all was when he didn't cough he sat against the pillow and never spoke or answered, or even made as if he heard. Only he looked offended.

"It's not your poor old gran's doing it, my lovey," said old Ma Parker, patting back the damp hair from his scarlet ears. But Lennie moved his head and edged away. Dreadfully offended with her he looked—and solemn. He bent his head and looked at her sideways as though he couldn't have believed it of his gran.

But at the last . . . Ma Parker threw the counterpane over the bed. No, she simply couldn't think about it. It was too much—she'd had too much in her life to bear. She'd borne it up till now, she'd kept herself to herself, and never once had she been seen to cry. Never by a living soul. Not even her own children had seen Ma break down. She'd kept a proud face always. But now! Lennie gone—what had she? She had nothing. He was all she'd got from life, and now he was took too. Why must it all have happened to me? she wondered. "What have I done?" said old Ma Parker. "What have I done?"

As she said those words she suddenly let fall her brush. She found herself in the kitchen. Her misery was so terrible that she pinned on her hat, put on her jacket and walked out of the flat like a person in a dream. She did not know what she was doing. She was like a person so dazed by the horror of what has happened that he walks away—anywhere, as though by walking away he could escape. . . .

Katherine Mansfield, LIFE OF MA PARKER

E Write a description of one of the following.

1 The strangest person I have ever met

2 My grandmother *or* My grandfather

3 The thoughts of someone waiting for news or for an important letter

4 Someone who feels lonely or left out

5 The shopkeeper *or* The nurse *or* The gardener.

14 ◆ Places

As with people, you may wish to establish **the setting of a story or a piece of personal writing** in a few phrases or sentences. Here are some approaches to consider:

- Pick out specific and striking details
- Colour the account by showing it through the eyes of a particular character or by showing how it reflects the character's mood
- Describe details that appeal to the senses – sight, hearing, touch, taste, smell
- Use figurative language to create vivid comparisons.

These are the points to concentrate on when writing a piece that is specifically **a description** of a place. You need also to ensure that your description has a structure and a shape. You could consider approaches like these:

- A panoramic view, moving from left to right of the scene
- An account that covers the scene over a number of hours – from morning to evening, for instance
- Using contrast – for example, the same scene when crowded and when quiet, or during the day and at night, or in summer and in winter
- An account seen from the point of view of two different and contrasted characters, or from the point of view of a character in two different moods.

A Examine the following passages. Comment on the methods used by the writers and on how effective their descriptions are.

1 Wednesday morning was dawning when I looked out of the window. The winking lights upon the bridges were already pale. The coming sun was like a marsh of fire on the horizon. The river, still dark and mysterious, was spanned by bridges that were turning coldly grey, with here and there at top a warm touch from the burning in the sky. As I looked along the clustered roofs, with church towers and spires shooting into the unusually clear sky, the sun rose up, and a veil seemed to be drawn from the river, and millions of sparkles burst out upon its waters. From me, too, a veil seemed to be drawn, and I felt strong and well.

Charles Dickens, GREAT EXPECTATIONS

2

That kitchen, worn by our boots and lives, was scruffy, warm and low, whose fuss of furniture seemed never the same but was shuffled around each day. A black grate crackled with coal and beech-twigs; towels toasted on the guard; the mantel was littered with fine old china, horse brasses and freak potatoes. On the floor were strips of muddy matting, the windows were choked with plants, the walls supported clocks and calendars, and smoky fungus ran over the ceilings. There were also six tables of different sizes, some armchairs gapingly stuffed, boxes, stools and unravelling baskets, books and papers on every chair, a sofa for cats, a harmonium for coats, and a piano for dust and photographs. These were the shapes of our kitchen landscape, the rocks of our submarine life, each object worn smooth by our constant nuzzling, or encrusted by lively barnacles, relics of birthdays and dead relations, wrecks of furniture long since foundered, all silted deep by mother's newspapers which the years piled round on the floor.

Laurie Lee, CIDER WITH ROSIE

3

One scene especially lingers in my mind. A frightful patch of waste ground (somehow, up there, a patch of waste ground attains a squalor that would be impossible even in London) trampled bare of grass and littered with newspapers and old saucepans. To the right an isolated row of gaunt four-roomed houses, dark red, blackened by smoke. To the left an interminable vista of factory chimneys, chimney upon chimney, fading away into a dim blackish haze. Behind me a railway embankment made of the slag from furnaces. In front, across the patch of waste ground, a cubical building of red and yellow brick, with the sign 'Thomas Grocock, Haulage Contractor'.

At night, when you cannot see the hideous shapes of the houses and the blackness of everything, a town like Sheffield assumes a kind of sinister magnificence. Sometimes the drifts of smoke are rosy with sulphur, and serrated flames, like circular saws, squeeze themselves out from beneath the cowls of the foundry chimneys. Through the open doors of the foundries you see fiery serpents of iron being hauled to and fro by redlit boys, and you hear the whizz and thump of steam hammers and the scream of the iron under the blow.

George Orwell, THE ROAD TO WIGAN PIER

4

The main street was a battleground in which the town had tried to fight the storm and had lost. It was a battleground littered with ruins, with tangled roofing iron, shattered cement sheets, weatherboards, rafters and sections of walls. Something crazy had smashed through the town, determined to destroy everything. That was how it looked. That was how it seemed.

Ivan Southall, HILLS END

5

This is the meat and poultry and bread market. There are stalls of new, various-shaped bread, brown and bright: there are tiny stalls of marvellous native cakes, which I want to taste: there is a great deal of meat and kid: and there are stalls of cheese, all shapes, all whitenesses, all the cream colours, on into daffodil yellow. Goat's cheese, sheep's cheese, Swiss cheese, Parmeggiano, stracchino, caciocavallo, torolone, how many cheeses I don't know the name of! . . . There are splendid piles of salted black olives, and huge bowls of green salted olives. There are chickens and ducks and wildfowl. There is mortadella, the enormous Bologna sausage, thick as a church pillar: and there are various sorts of smaller sausage, salami, to be eaten in slices. A wonderful abundance of food, glowing and shining.

D.H. Lawrence, SEA AND SARDINIA

B Write sentences, one for each, that effectively describe the following: a house, a room, a beach, a hill, a street.

C Examine the following description. What particular aspects of the scene does the writer concentrate on? Does the piece have a structure and a shape?

Gorbals Cross was a large open space, roughly circular, a little way along Gorbals Street to the south of the River Clyde, where Norfolk Street came in at right angles from the west and became Ballater Street to the east of the crossing. Gorbals Street stretched about a third of a mile, from within sight of Dixon's Blazes at its southern end up to the Clyde at the Victoria Bridge. Gorbals Cross was also the name of the square granite monument in the middle of the open space. At each corner of its central block a plinth jutted out, supporting a Doric column from the capital of which a scrolled buttress curved inwards to where, high on one face of the main block, were the city's arms; above was a clock with a white dial on each of the tower's four sides, the whole topped by a little four-sided stepped pyramid with a decorated cross of wrought iron at its peak. The embrasures between the plinths had stone ledges or benches, little open air drawing rooms where in fine weather men in cloth caps and mufflers smoked and talked. In one of them, stone steps led up to a bronze drinking fountain with two iron beakers hanging on heavy chains on either side of its basin.

The space occupied by the monument and the broad pavement surrounding it was some twenty-five feet in diameter. At the outer perimeter of the crossing, like an enclosing wall, rose black tenement buildings in the handsome classical style favoured in their epoch, the middle years of the nineteenth century.

Tram rails set into the smooth grey cobbles took a wide curve round the monument. As the tall glass-sided vehicles moved sedately in their circuit their wheels grated on the metal with a sonorous, brassy note that reverberated from the walls of the close ring of tenements, and rang in the mind like the sustained call of a horn in a far valley. In the quiet hours late at night and in the early morning you could imagine that the call came from a lonely oracle sending a message to the world. As it faded, taken up perhaps in another valley, and another, you felt its continuing power even in the ensuing silence. One day its meaning would come plainly through the mists. Long years afterwards, wherever you were in the world, you had only to think back to that time, and the poignant and questioning call vibrated in your head once again.

The day would come when the trams stopped. The rails would be dug up from the cobbles. But the horn note in the far valley would still sound in one's heart.

As long as motor vehicles shared the streets with many horse drawn carts and vans, till about 1930, traffic was not heavy, and moved with convenient slowness. People walked unhurriedly over to the Cross from the periphery, took a drink of water from the fountain, stood and stared, passed the time of day with friends. They took one of the large iron beakers, pitted and dented from years of rough use, and pressed its rim against a button under the spout to release a jet of sparkling water, crisply refreshing, that came from Loch Katrine in the Trossachs, some forty miles to the north of Glasgow.

I had never seen Loch Katrine, but the name had magical power. It conjured up steel engravings of *The Lady of the Lake*, remembered from English lessons at school, gothic scenes of wild crags and dark groves full of mystery, and figures on the Silver Strand moving in their romantic destinies – thoughts of the earth spirits. In dour contrast was the inscription, in gold letters beneath the coat of arms, that met your eye as you drank from the beaker: 'Let

Glasgow flourish', a shortened version of the City's motto: 'Lord let Glasgow flourish through the preaching of thy Word and praising thy Name'.

Did they want us to believe that religion was good for business? Did they themselves believe it? They. Them. The people who had mastery over the likes of us.

Children played on the uneven paving surrounding the monument. Grown-ups lingered there and talked and watched the passing scene, or called to friends on the far perimeter; and the latter might thread their way through the traffic to join them. As the years went by and motor traffic filled the streets more and more, there were demands to have the Cross removed – from business interests arguing for faster transport, and do-gooders, mainly from the better-off parts of the city, who felt that the Gorbals should be shorn of its old ways and appearance. In 1932 the City Fathers did have it taken away – not for any of these reasons, it was said, but because it led to accidents by tempting people to wander over to it across the path of the now faster-moving vehicles.

For a long time Gorbals folk behaved as if this had not happened. They returned again and again, halted at the periphery of the crossing and stared with unbelief at the empty place in the centre; turned and paced about restlessly, deprived of a mysterious comfort, vital but indefinable. The monument had been the focus of many emotions and many associations of ideas, a source of answers to myriad unspoken questions; it had drawn them close, the hub of a moving wheel, its magic acknowledged, or rather felt, only in retrospect, after it had gone.

No one could put the loss fittingly into words. Few were inclined to dwell on it. It strengthened the conviction that the world, 'they', cared not a scrap for the feelings of people without power.

Ralph Glasser, GROWING UP IN THE GORBALS

D Write a description suggested by one of the following.

1   The waste ground

2   You could see for miles and miles

3   The street market

4   After the storm

5   When winter gives way to spring.

15◆Events

When writing an account of an event, you could use many of the approaches suggested for writing about people and places (see Chapters 13 and 14). You should try to:

- Use plenty of specific and concrete detail

- Describe people and places in an interesting way

- Describe your feelings and thoughts or those of your observer where appropriate

- Use figurative language to make your description more precise and vivid

- Adopt a particular point of view – for example, that of a cynic or an enthusiast, or someone trying a taste, sport, etc., for the first time, if that is appropriate

- See that your account has a definite structure and shape.

Following the sequence of actions of an event step by step can help to provide you with a structure and a shape – though it would be possible to start your account in the middle or at the end and then go back to the beginning. Whichever method you choose, it is important to make sure that the various stages of what is happening are made clear to the reader.

A Study the following accounts of events. Consider how clearly the sequence of actions is presented, whether or not the account has a structure and shape, and how interestingly the event is described.

The cars slowly moved forward to the waiting cross-channel ferry, as the great jaws at the stern of the vessel gobbled up the line of vehicles. Inside was a long, low, noisy hold; and slowly the cars were packed in one by one. The jaws closed. The engines started to throb, and at first the whole vessel pulsated as the engines began to make headway.

Upstairs, in the dining compartment, people were sleeping or just sitting quietly. Gradually all noises died away and just the booming of the engines, or an occasional snore could be heard.

On deck it was cold, and windy. People sat wrapped in blankets, sitting on one of the numerous benches, just staring into the black water. At the bows of the ship the spray hovered in the biting wind, a taste of salt comes to your mouth. The wind howled and whistled through the many ropes and cables.

Down below it is quiet, almost another world completely. Time passes; it's gradually beginning to get light. Movement starts, people getting the breakfast from the bar. The whole boat seems to come alive again. Gradually, the noise from the land gets louder. Seagulls begin to screech. Finally, you reach Boulogne harbour and the seamen start the slow process of getting the cars out, engines warm up, the noise and excitement start and at last you're in the fresh French air.

Bernard Jones, CHANNEL CROSSING

2

Enough tears for an old soak

By COLIN MALAM
Wolves 1, Cardiff 4

AT THE END of this extra-ordinary match, the skies opened and the rain fell in buckets on Molineux. Coming after a dry, sunny afternoon, the deluge was as dramatic and unexpected as what had just happened on the field.

Perhaps it was all those Wolves' heroes of the past shedding a tear over the succession of horrendous defensive errors that brought a rare home defeat and threatened the club's leadership of the Fourth Division.

Cardiff's victory, the first here by a visiting team since another Welsh side, Wrexham, won 2-0 on November 28, reduced the gap between themselves and Wolves from six points to just three.

As this was only Wolves' second defeat in 17 matches, they must have been doing something right up to now. Whatever it was, though, they showed little of it in any

department on the day, ironi-cally manager Graham Turner was voted Fourth Division Manager of the Month.

In addition to their fragility in defence, Wolves were far too dependent in attack on Steve Bull, the big, rawbone striker. Bull, who never stops running or trying and is capable of unsuspected flashes of skill, duly got a goal, his 27th of the season.

Frankly, neither side had played well up to the 63rd minute. What brought the play sharply to life was enterprising work by Curtis and McDer-mott on the Cardiff left. When Gilligan drove McDermott's centre firmly at the net, two Wolves defenders battled to clear it off the line, but the linesman flagged unhesitat-ingly for a goal.

Three minutes later, Bartlett made amends for his first-half miss, and another at the start of the second half, by using his pace to get behind the Wolves' defence on the right. He pulled the ball back precisely and

Wimbleton steered it sweetly home.

With Wolves beginning to fall apart, Gilligan then hit a post from two yards when Bartlett's pass made it easier to score. So, when Bull cut Cardiff's lead to a single goal by pouncing on a loose ball and shooting on the turn after 72 minutes, it seemed Wolves were right back in the game.

Gilligan shattered that illu-sion by slotting in Cardiff's third goal, his 19th of the season, from a narrow angle following a mistake by Clarke nine minutes from the end.

For Wolves, it was not simply a matter of keeping the score down, so there was a sigh of relief all round when Ken-dall rushed out to deny Bartlett.

There were no pats on the back for the Wolves' keeper in the 86th minute, though. Somehow, he managed to let the ball slip through his hands and legs and over the line when Wimbleton made an angle for himself on the byline and shot.

THE SUNDAY TELEGRAPH

72

3

I had barely begun my first cup of coffee when I heard a hooter sound the alarm, six long blasts—and almost at once the telephone rang. It was George Conway, secretary of the Medical Aid Society. Briefly he told me that a disaster had occurred in the Ystfad Colliery at Pengelly across the mountain; they had sent out a routine call for aid. Would I go over at once?

Hastily, I swallowed a few mouthfuls of food, finished my coffee and set off across the ridge on my motor bike. It was no more than two miles by mountain track to Pengelly, and I reached the village in less than five minutes. Yet already the news of the calamity was travelling through the narrow streets. Doors in the terraces were open, men and women rushing downhill toward the colliery. As they ran, more ran with them. They ran as if they could not help themselves, as if the pit had suddenly become a magnet drawing them irresistibly toward it.

When I arrived, five hundred men and women had gathered on the outskirts of the pit yard, and there were more outside. They stood in silence, the women mostly in shawls, the men without overcoats. It had been snowing here and their figures were very black against the white snow. They stood like some vast chorus, massed in silence under the clear sky. They were not the actors in the drama, but they were of it none the less.

Eight o'clock had just struck when I pushed my way into the pit yard and entered the wooden colliery office, where a number of the surface crew, all in their working clothes, were collected. The mine manager, Dai Jenkins, whom I knew well, was there with his deputy, Tom Lewis, looking at the crowd. As I entered the deputy was saying:

'Will I have the yard gates shut?'

'No,' answered the other. 'Have a fire lighted in the yard, a large fire. It's cold for them standing there, and God knows they may stand long enough.'

In the pause which followed I asked what had happened. At first Jenkins did not seem to hear, then, turning upon me his strained and harassed gaze, he told me that water had broken into the pit from the old workings. Both main shafts were flooded and both morning shifts, sixty-one men in all, were entombed. They were waiting for the first rescue party to bring heavy pumping equipment from the emergency centre at Gilfach. They could not tell how things were underground, having lost all contact with the trapped men. They could only wait for the moment, until the rescue party arrived. As he spoke, more people came crowding into the office—two of the underviewers, a young inspector of mines, another colliery manager from further down the valley, and a party of volunteers from the neighbouring colliery. There was no confusion, no babble of voices, but an attitude of such deep gravity it filled me with foreboding.

Suddenly, in the midst of this tense expectancy, the mine telephone whirred—not the public service instrument upon the manager's desk, but the wall attachment of the colliery system which communicated only with the underground workings. Instantly, there was a mortal silence, then, in three strides, Jenkins was at the phone. He spun the little handle violently, lifted the receiver.

'Hello, hello!' Then his face paled, he half turned to the other 'My God . . . it's Roberts!'

At first I did not understand. Then I realized, with a contraction of my heart, that a voice, the voice of a man not yet dead, was rising out of the dark tomb of the flooded mine, fleeing in despairing hope over waterlogged wires to us, on the surface, two miles away.

'Hello, hello!' Jenkins was listening now, he listened for three minutes with strained intentness, then rapidly, in a hard clear voice, he began to speak. 'Listen to me, Roberts, bach. You must make for the old Penygroes shaft. You can't come out this way—both shafts are water-sealed, and it may be days before we clear them. You must travel the old workings. Go right up the slant. Break through the frame dam at the top east side. That takes you into the upper level of the old workings. Don't be afraid of water, that's all in the bottom levels. Go along the road, it's all main road, don't take the trenches nor the right dip, keep bearing due east for fifteen hundred yards until you strike the old Penygroes shaft.'

A thick, roaring noise came over the wire, audible in the room, and Jenkins' voice rose feverishly to a shout.

'Do you hear me? The rescue party will meet you there. Do you hear me?' But his words were lost as a water blast tore out the wires and left the instrument dead in his hand. He let it fall—it swung dangling, while he stood there, bowed, motionless.

A.J. Cronin, ADVENTURES IN TWO WORLDS

B Write a description of one of the following events:

1   The concert *or* The big match
2   The day the school was on show
3   Field trip
4   The accident
5   The visit of someone famous.

16 ◆ An Argument

When writing an essay supporting or attacking a particular argument, you have to put your case as persuasively as possible so as to convince your readers. Here are some suggestions that could help.

1   Think up as many arguments as you can to support your case. Do not just rely on one or two points. Consider also factors that could weaken your case and work out arguments to counter them.

2   Support your views with evidence such as statistics, illustrations, examples, details, topical references, personal experience, incidents taken from television and newspapers. Do not simply make general statements.

3   Try to avoid defective arguments such as generalisations, assumptions, false emotional appeals, appealing to prejudice, and so on. (See *Reading and Understanding*, Chapter 18, 'Defective Arguments'.)

4   Use analogies and figurative language where these would help to make the reader see your argument in a new or striking light.

5   Plan and organise your essay before you begin. Make notes of the points you are going to make and the evidence you are going to use.

6   Present your points in the most effective order. You might begin with the most important or you might lead up to the most important as the climax of your argument.

7   Use an opening that catches the reader's attention and an ending that hammers your argument home or leaves your reader with something to think about. (See Chapter 9, 'Opening and Ending'.)

A   Consider the following argument against boxing. How much evidence in support of his view does the writer give? How much use is made of emotional appeal? How much space is devoted to undermining the opposite view?

They call it the noble art. But what is noble about two men slugging away at each other until one of them is unconscious on the canvas while hundreds of people, safe in their seats, roar and shriek for blood, and a few others, without lifting a fist, can pour money into their bank deposits?

If you have ever seen a boxer after a bout, you would never call boxing noble. You must have seen those close-ups on television – those bleary half-shut eyes, those bruised thickened lips, that puffy battered flesh, the blood pouring from cuts around the eyes. It is degrading to think that a man has been prepared to put up with that kind of punishment in the name of sport and as a means of making a living. It is degrading to think that it was another man who inflicted that pain and punishment on him for the same reasons.

But it goes beyond a battered face and a loss of dignity. Recently, the boxer Steve Watt died in the ring, and pressure rose again for the sport to be banned. And rightly so. What kind of sport is it that ends in a man's death? The chief medical officer for the British Boxing Board of Control has pointed out that since 1948 there have been only twelve deaths within the game and has said, 'If only every sport could be as safe as that.'

It is true that people die in motor racing or climbing mountains. But there is a difference. In those sports, people are pitting themselves against speed or natural hazards. They are not being pounded to death by their fellow men for the entertainment of the masses.

In any case, it's not simply a case of deaths. How many boxers have had to retire into a premature senile old age because of brain damage? Recent film on television of Mohammed Ali was shocking. Someone who had once been a vital quip-a-minute young man has become a bewildered inarticulate zombie. Constantly being beaten about the head by men determined to knock you out is bound to have some effect.

And there is evidence to prove it. The British Medical Association working party on boxing has stated that X-ray brain scanning shows beyond doubt that permanent brain damage commonly occurs in men who box. Doctors may differ in their opinions, but the fact that the BMA has this kind of evidence and is campaigning to have boxing banned must carry a lot of weight.

It's not just the dangers of boxing itself that cause concern. It is also the whole atmosphere that surrounds it. That crowds of people – men and women – can cheer and get excited at the sight of two men doing their best to hurt and damage each other is sickening. It is uncivilised. It is little better than the Roman gladiatorial fights to the death which history and society condemned long ago.

It has been argued in favour of boxing that it is one of the few ways in which a working-class lad can achieve fame and fortune. But for how many is this true? One in a million? More typical is the case of Randy Turpin, once a world champion, who ended up a drunk and practically destitute and finally committed suicide.

No, it's not the boxers who make the money, it's the promoters. With their betting and big deals and Mafia organisations, they're the ones who go laughing all the way to the bank. And when one of their boxers is finished, his brains beaten to a pulp, they drop him without a backward glance and seize on someone else to exploit.

'What a piece of work is a man!' says Shakespeare in *Hamlet*. 'How noble in reason! how infinite in faculty! in form, in moving, how express and admirable! in action how like an angel! in apprehension how like a god! the beauty of the world! the paragon of animals!'

The next time you see a boxing match on television, with two exhausted men, faces bruised and bloodied, hanging on to each other because their legs are giving way, being jeered at by the crowd and urged on to show them some action, think of that. Do boxers live up to this view of what man is or ought to be? There is more dignity in sweeping roads.

B Consider the following argument against vivisection. What main points does the writer make? What evidence does he use to support his view? Does he use emotional appeal fairly? How convincing do you find his argument?

The RSPCA says that about 5,000,000 animals are experimented on every year in Britain. That includes birds, dogs, cats, frogs, rats, mice, monkeys and others. Some are bred especially for the purpose, others are captured in the wild. They are given electric shocks, infected with diseases, fed with poisons, chemicals are dripped into their eyes, surgery is performed on them, they are subjected to radiation, they have tumours implanted in their bodies, tiny infants are deprived of their mothers . . . and so on and on.

And yet this suffering is unnecessary! There are alternatives, far better alternatives. Take the claims for medical research. The suffering this causes actually has the opposite effect to what the experimenters are trying to achieve.

Vivisectionists experiment on animals to produce drugs, antidotes and antitoxins. Almost every day, it seems, another drug is banned, because so many have side-effects. Those that remain repress symptoms without giving credence to the cause that gave rise to them.

A symptom, like a headache or other pain, is merely the body's warning that something deeper needs to be looked at. By applying drugs to symptoms, they are not curing the root cause, so the problem returns. So, animal experimentation, it can be argued actually perpetuates disease.

Millions of people are now turning towards Alternative Medicine, like homoeopathy which, without resort to vivisection, treats the whole body.

It is rapidly being acknowledged that all diseases start in the mind. The modern condition often provokes a hardness of mind and a blinkered attitude towards vivisection and the suffering of others.

Those attitudes *create* disease. I must stress that this is not a religious fanatic's point of view. I am not trying to drum up a punishment inflicted on mankind. It's just a simple scientific equation. As we tolerate vivisection, so we will eventually be made to pay. I believe that a bad state of mind eventually percolates into the body, and gets it into a like state.

I can't think of any terms low enough to describe my feeling about using animals to test the safety of cosmetics. It is totally indefensible. It is appalling that such suffering should be caused for pure vanity. Man has the power to discriminate, animals don't. For us consciously to titillate our vanity while condoning and financing the extremes of agony that are experienced in these animal concentration camps is disgraceful.

It is no argument to say that it is better for an animal to suffer than for a child to lose an eye through a toxic product. There are plenty of ways of making cosmetics safely that don't involve animals at all. There's a firm called Beauty Without Cruelty which has a complete range of cosmetics formulated safely, without harming helpless creatures in the process.

Money is always at the bottom of everything. It talks louder than the people who want to say 'no' to vivisection. They have never had the financial backing to fight those who want to perpetuate their own profits and don't mind causing distress and agony along the way. But at last there is one way that money can be used on our side.

Because of the cosmetic and commercial uses for whale products, these creatures have been almost wiped out, and in great agony. But now a plant called the jojoba is being harvested from the desert. The jojoba's oil is not just superior to a whale's, but it can also be used as food, polishes and in a whole host of industrial processes. And its bean is superior in every way to everything that was once taken from the whale's or any other animal's body.

Now that the International Whaling Commission is trying to bring about a complete ban on whaling, I would be very happy if people invested in the jojoba and crops like it, so that people will profit from things which are grown rather than from animals which are tortured and killed. I'm sure the jojoba is the beginning of a brand-new attitude, generated by good sense and, let's face it, high profits.

Although it may not sound like it, I've given up campaigning against vivisection. It doesn't work. You can't change the world. All you can do is carry on working yourself and try to change people's attitudes by your example.

I hope that doesn't sound sanctimonious. It starts with *you*, the person reading this article, saying: 'I won't buy anything that has involved the suffering of animals.' You do that and the anti-vivisection movement will grow from within and suffering will stop. And you will feel a lot better, too.

Martin Shaw, TV TIMES

(For an argument in favour of vivisection, see *Oral Communication*, Chapter 2, 'Speaking'.)

C Consider the following analogies. How effective do you think each would be in an argument? Justify your view.

1 Advertising is like the rattling of a stick inside a swill bucket.

George Orwell

2 Critics are like brushers of noblemen's clothes.

Sir Henry Wotton

3 Education is like a Chinese meal: a succession of short courses and you never quite finish any of them.

Nicholas Coleridge

4 The House of Lords is like a perfect eventide home.

Lady Stocks

5 Being a lawyer is like being a bottle of ketchup in a restaurant that specialises in bad steaks. It covers a multitude of sins.

Jerome Weidman

6 Golf is like a love affair: if you don't take it seriously it's no fun; if you do take it seriously it breaks your heart.

Arnold Daly

7 Marriage is like pleading guilty for an indefinite sentence. Without parole.

John Mortimer

8 Disneyland is like being force-fed candy floss.

Ronnie Paris

9 Life is like eating artichokes – you've got to go through so much to get so little.

T. A. Dorgan

10 A woman's preaching is like a dog's walking on his hinder legs. It is not done well, but you are surprised to find it done at all.

Samuel Johnson

D Consider the following arguments about space exploration. Which do you find the most convincing? What evidence can you find to support these arguments and what further arguments can you find? Would you support or oppose space exploration?

1 Space exploration increases man's knowledge of the universe.

2 Rivalry between nations over space exploration could lead to violence and war.

3 It is better for nations to vie with each other over space exploration than to confront each other aggressively on earth.

4 The increasing complexity of space exploration means a greater possibility of disaster and danger to human life.

5 Space exploration increases the national prestige of those states that take part and succeed.

6 Space exploration provides and develops technical advances which can be used to improve industrial technology and the quality of life on earth.

7 The money used on space exploration would be better used to relieve poverty and famine on earth and improve living conditions here.

8 Space exploration provides an opportunity for people to show and expand their spirit of adventure.

9 Trying to find out more about space is defying the laws of God and Nature.

10 The financial cost of space exploration is greater than any advantages that may result from it.

E Write an essay giving your arguments for or against one of the following:

1 Space exploration

2 Abortion

3 Advertising on BBC

4 Sunday opening of pubs

5 A subject of your own choice about which you feel strongly.

17◆Response to Stimuli

Stimuli of various kinds can often help to get the mind moving and encourage ideas for writing. A photograph, a painting, a few bars of music, a single word, an image in a poem, a sudden sound, an unusual object that you can touch and examine – all these can stimulate thoughts and ideas. Even a strange scent or the taste of something can evoke memories of different situations. There is the famous example of the French novelist Marcel Proust who tells in *Remembrance of Things Past* how the taste of a little 'madeleine' cake dipped in tea brought back memories of his childhood.

You have to allow the stimulus a chance to work. You have to let your mind go free so that any associations suggested by the stimulus can enter and expand.

For instance, the word 'bread' might suggest ways in which bread has become a symbol for basic survival through the centuries, or it may suggest a story about a starving family.

This image from a poem by Edward Thomas

> The new moon hangs like an ivory bugle
> In the naked frosty blue

could set you off on a description of a frosty night, or could create the setting for a story.

A shocked face in a photograph may remind you of an occasion when you felt like that, or you may be drawn into the person's situation and try to work out what has happened.

A Choose one of the following and write about anything it suggests to you.

1 Panic

2 Sleep

3 Horses

4 Night

5 Peace

B Choose one of the following and write about anything suggested to you.

1

He knew that coastline – no man better –
Knew all its rocks and currents, like the veins
And knuckles on the brown back of his hand.

Jon Stallworthy

2

The whoop of a boy, the thud of a hoof,
The rattle of rain on a galvanised roof,
The hubbub of traffic, the roar of a train,
The throb of machinery numbing the brain.

Jessie Pope

3

The place smelt old, of things too long kept shut,
The smell of absences where shadows come
That can't be polished.

Elizabeth Jennings

4

The night tinkles like ice in glasses,
Leaves are glued to the pavement with frost.

Norman MacCaig

5

Her mother hears the clock; her father sighs,
Takes off his boots: she's late tonight.

David Holbrook

C Choose one of the following and write about anything suggested to you.

1

Photographer MICHAEL PATTISON   DAILY TELEGRAPH

2

THE GUARDIAN

3

Photographer PHILIP WOLMUTH

4

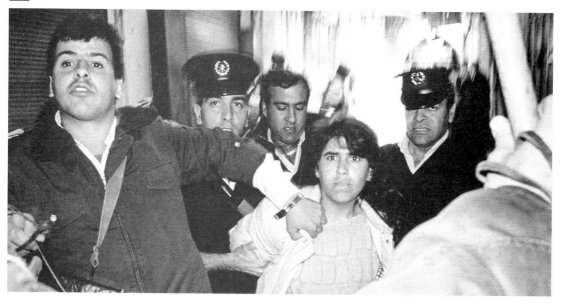

Photographer BOB GANNON

18◆Responding to Reading

You are likely to be asked to provide some writing in your coursework that shows a response to something you have read. This could be literary (a novel, a play, a poem) or non-literary (a newspaper article, a report, an advertisement). In either case, what is wanted are your thoughts about the piece and your reactions to it.

It could help if you consider the piece in the following four stages.

1   What is the writer saying?   In other words, what is the piece about? If it is a story, you have to examine things like characters, plot and setting. If it is an argument, you have to examine the points the writer is making. The point of view, the underlying theme and the structure can also be important in helping you to work out the meaning.

2   How is the writer saying it?   In other words, what methods is the writer using to get his or her point across. Things like characters, plot, setting, point of view, theme and structure could also be relevant here. But you would also examine things like the tone and language used, figurative language, the sentence structure and paragraphing, the use of dialogue.

3   How successful is the writer?   In other words, is the piece effective and does it work? Again, many of the factors already mentioned need to be considered, and the audience for which the piece is intended also has a bearing. For instance, are the tone and language appropriate for the theme and the audience? Do the sentence structure and paragraphing help to make the meaning more effective?

4   What is your own response?   After working through the previous stages, you should be in a position to give a personal response to the piece. For instance, you should be able to say whether you found a story or a poem convincing or moving, or an argument persuasive, and say why. You may find that the piece strikes a chord in your own experience, or it may illuminate some aspect of life or human relationships in a way that you had not previously thought of.

It can help to discuss a piece of writing in groups or as a class. Other people's ideas can often stimulate ideas of your own. But if you do discuss the piece, this should be stated on the sheet on which you do your own writing. |

Sometimes for coursework you are required to write a piece in controlled classroom conditions. That is, you are required to work on your own in a quiet atmosphere for a specified length of time. Responding to reading is something which could well be done in controlled classroom conditions.

A Write about the following poem. In your account, describe what happens in the poem, the methods the poet uses to make the scene vivid, and the thoughts and feelings the poet leaves you with at the end. Write at least 400 words. (If you are writing in controlled classroom conditions, allow one hour for the writing.)

Gunpowder Plot

For days these curious cardboard buds have lain
In brightly coloured boxes. Soon the night
Will come. We pray there'll be no sullen rain
To make these magic orchids flame less bright.

Now in the garden's darkness they begin
To flower: the frenzied whizz of Catherine-wheel
Puts forth its fiery petals and the thin
Rocket soars to burst upon the steel

Bulwark of a cloud. And then the guy,
Absurdly human phoenix, is again
Gulped by greedy flames: the harvest sky
Is flecked with threshed and glittering golden grain.

'Uncle! A cannon! Watch me as I light it!'
The women helter-skelter, squealing high,
Retreat; the paper fuse is quickly lit,
A cat-like hiss and spit of fire, a sly

Falter, then the air is shocked with blast.
The cannon bangs and in my nostrils drifts
A bitter scent that brings the lurking past
Lurching to my side. The present shifts,

Allows a ten-year memory to walk
Unhindered now; and so I'm forced to hear
The banshee howl of mortar and the talk
Of men who died; am forced to taste my fear.

I listen for a moment to the guns,
The torn earth's grunts, recalling how I prayed.
The past retreats. I hear a corpse's sons –
'Who's scared of bangers?' 'Uncle! John's afraid!'

Vernon Scannell

B Give your views on the following short story. Write at least 400 words. (If you are writing in controlled classroom conditions, allow one hour for the writing.)

Jamaican Fragment

Every day I walk a half-mile from my home to the tramcar lines in the morning, and from the lines to my home in the evening. The walk is pleasant. The road on either side is flanked by red- and green-roofed bungalows, green lawns and gardens. The exercise is good for me and now and then I learn something from a little incident.

One morning, about half-way between my front gate and the tram track, I noticed two little boys playing in the garden of one of the more modest cottages. They were both very little boys, one was four years old perhaps, the other five. The bigger of the two was a sturdy youngster, very dark, with a mat of coarse hair on his head and coal-black eyes. He was definitely a little Jamaican—a strong little Jamaican. The other little fellow was smaller, but also sturdy—he was white, with hazel eyes and light-brown hair. Both were dressed in blue shirts and khaki pants: they wore no shoes and their feet were muddy. They were not conscious of my standing there watching them; they played on. The game, if it could be called a game, was not elaborate. The little white boy strode imperiously up and down and every now and then shouted imperiously at his bigger playmate. The little brown boy shuffled along quietly behind him and did what he was told.

"Pick up that stick!" The dark boy picked it up.

"Jump into the flowers!" The dark boy jumped.

"Get me some water!" The dark boy ran inside. The white boy sat down on the lawn.

I was amazed. Here before my eyes, a white baby, for they were little more than babies, was imposing his will upon a little black boy. And the little black boy submitted. I puzzled within myself as I went down the road. Could it be that the little dark boy was the son of a servant in the home and therefore had to do the white boy's bidding? No. They were obviously dressed alike, the little dark boy was of equal class with his playmate. No. They were playmates, the little dark boy was a neighbour's child. I was sure of that. Then how was it that he obeyed so faithfully the white boy's orders? Was it that even at his early age he sensed that in his own country he would be at the white man's beck and call? Could he

in such youth divine a difference between himself and the white boy? And did the little white youngster so young, such a baby, realize that he would grow to dominate the black man? Was there an indefinable quality in the white man that enabled his baby, smaller and younger than his playmate, to make him his slave? Was there really some difference between a white man and a black man? Something that made the white superior? I could find no answer. I could not bring myself to believe such a thing, and yet, with my own eyes I had seen a little dark boy take orders from a little white boy—a little white boy obviously his social equal, and younger and smaller. Were we as a race really inferior? So inferior that even in our infancy we realized our deficiencies, and accepted a position as the white man's servant?

For a whole day I puzzled over this problem. For a whole day my faith in my people was shaken. When I passed that afternoon the little boys were not there. That evening I thought deeply on the subject.

The next morning the boys were there again, and a man was standing at the gate watching them. I stopped and looked, just to see what the white boy was making his little servant do. To my utter astonishment the little dark boy was striding imperiously up and down the lawn, while the white youngster walked abjectly behind him.

"Get me a banana!" The little white boy ran into the house and reappeared shortly with a banana. "Peel it for me!" The little white boy skinned the banana and handed it to his dark master.

I saw it now. This was indeed a game, a game I had played as a child. Each boy took it in turn every alternate day to be the boss, the other the slave. It had been great fun to me as a youngster. I smiled as I remembered. I looked at the man standing by the gate. He was a white man. I remembered what I had thought yesterday. He, no doubt, I thought to myself, was wondering if the black race is superior to the white. I laughed gently to myself. How silly grown-ups are, how clever we are, how wonderfully able we are to impute deep motives to childish actions! How suspicious we are when we have been warped by prejudice! This man, I said to myself, will puzzle all day on whether the blacks will eventually arise and rule the world because he thinks he sees a little black boy realizing at a tender age his superiority over the white. I will save him his puzzle. I will explain it to him. I went across to him.

"I know what you're thinking," I said. "You're thinking that maybe the black race is superior to the

white, because you just saw the little dark youngster on the lawn ordering the little white boy around. Don't think that, it's a game they play. Alternate days one is boss, the other the servant. It's a grand game. I used to play it and maybe so did you. Yesterday I saw the little white boy bossing the dark one and I worried all day over the dark boy's realization of his inferiority so young in life! We are silly, we grown-ups, aren't we?"

The man was surprised at my outburst. He looked at me smiling.

"I know all about the game," he said. "The boys are brothers—my sons." He pointed to a handsome brown woman on the veranda who had just come out to call in the children. "That's my wife," he said.

I smiled. My spirit laughed within me. This is Jamaica, I said in my heart, this is my country—my people. I looked at the white man. He smiled at me. "We'll miss the tram if we don't hurry," he said.

A.L. Hendricks

C Write about the following newspaper report. Say what the report is about, describe how fairly and effectively the reporter presents the facts, and give your own views and experience on the subject. You should write at least 400 words. (If you are writing in controlled classroom conditions, allow one hour for the writing.)

Battle of the sexes at play

THE BATTLE between the sexes begins at nursery school according to Seamus Dunn and Valerie Morgan of the University of Ulster. They watched children aged between four and seven at play in four nursery or infant classrooms in Northern Ireland and found that the boys monopolised some toys and that the girls allowed the boys to dominate them.

The most popular toys were the bicycles, and the boys made sure that they got them – sometimes by intimidating other children. Girls who wanted to ride a bicycle did not challenge other children, but either waited until one was free or enlisted the help of the teacher. They then rode sedately about, but boys on bicycles were more likely to ram each other.

The sand tray and large construction toys were other high-status items. These toys often caused arguments about whose turn it was to use them. These arguments were almost always between boys and girls, and the boys almost always won – often through force. When the girls were asked why they gave up so easily, they were unable to say.

Even at such an early age, boys and girls strongly pre-ferred to play with members of their own sex. In one class, playing in the sand tray was highly popular and in struggles for possession, according to the researchers, most children knew clearly where their loyalties lay. "The boys can play in the sand," said one boy firmly, and when a girl approached he shouted: "No girls!" In another incident, four girls pushed a boy away whenever he approached the tray.

Much of the children's behaviour mirrored ultra-conventional roles for the sexes, especially in the play house. Girls were nurses and boys were doctors (although in real life a fair proportion of doctors are women); girls served meals to boys, made the tea and washed the dishes.

The teachers sometimes reinforced the patterns. "Serve the tea out nicely – show the boys how to do it properly. Your mummy doesn't do it like that," said one during a pretend tea party, when the boys were sitting at the table waiting to be served.

But the boys did not always observe the social niceties. The girls used play shops and houses for shopping, cooking meals and putting dolls to bed, but the boys would turn objects into whatever they wanted. Toy irons would become guns, saucepans were helmets, dolls' house furniture became military targets and the play house a climbing frame. Two boys, using a pair of sink taps as guns, and two women's hats as stetsons, set off to play cowboys.

Dunn and Morgan argue that it is through play that boys first learn to dominate girls, and they develop their creative skills by using the play materials as they want. This kind of early experience, Dunn and Morgan suggest, could contribute to the underachievement and lost career opportunities which hamper many girls in later life.

Caroline St-John Brooks, THE SUNDAY TIMES

D Write about a novel or a play you have read. Give your thoughts about it and your reactions to it.

E Write about a group of poems you have read. They could be by the same poet or be about the same subject. Say what the poems are about, describe the similiarities and/or differences between the poems and the ways they make their effects, and give your personal reactions to the poems.

19◆Directed Writing

You may select information from a piece of writing and then re-use this information in a piece of writing of your own which has a different purpose. For instance, you may read a newspaper article about a particularly dangerous road in your area. You may then write a letter to your local councillor complaining about this road and using information given in the article.

Directed writing is an exercise in which you are asked to select material from a piece of writing which you then use in a form that you are directed to use. It is partly an exercise in reading and understanding and partly an exercise in writing.

Here is some advice on how to set about it:

– Read the passage to get a general impression of it.

– Make sure you understand what information is going to be relevant to the task set.

– Read the passage again, identifying and isolating where this information is. It may help to make some notes of it.

– Make sure you understand the form that your own piece of writing is to take.

– Write your version, using the information in the form directed. Make sure you use language and tone that are appropriate to your purpose and the audience addressed.

A Billie Holiday was a black American blues singer of the 1930s. Write an account of the case described here as it might have appeared in a newspaper. Decide whether your newspaper is of the quality or tabloid variety. Use only information obtained from this extract.

It was called 'The United States of America versus Billie Holiday'. And that's just the way it felt.

They brought me into a courtroom in the US District Courthouse at Ninth and Market streets in Philly – only two blocks from the Earle Theatre where it had all begun eleven days before. But those two damn blocks seemed like the Atlantic Ocean. It was Tuesday, 27 May 1947.

Somebody read off the charge: 'On or about 16 May 1947, and divers dates theretofore in the Eastern District of Pennsylvania, Billie Holiday did receive,

conceal, carry and facilitate the transportation and concealment of . . . drugs . . . fraudulently imported and brought into the United States contrary to law, in violation of Section 174, Title 21, USCA.'

An assistant US district attorney opened. 'All right, Billie Holiday,' he said. 'You are charged with violation of the Narcotics Act and you have been shown a copy of the information and have indicated your desire to waive the presentation of an indictment by the Grand Jury. You are entitled to a lawyer.'

'I have none,' I said. And that was the

truth, I hadn't seen one, talked to one.

'Do you want a lawyer, Miss Holiday?' the DA asked.

'No,' I answered.

I didn't think there was anyone who would help me. And worse, I had been convinced that nobody *could* help me.

'Then this is a waiver of appointment of counsel if you will sign "Billie Holiday" on that line.'

They shoved me a pink paper to sign and I signed it.

I would have signed anything, no matter what. I hadn't eaten anything for a week. I couldn't even keep water down. Every time I tried to take a nap, some big old officer would come around and wake me up to sign something, make me dress, go to another office.

When it came time for me to appear in court I couldn't even walk. I was in no shape to go before the judge. So they agreed to give me a shot to keep me from getting sick. It turned out to be morphine.

Then the judge spoke up. 'Was this woman ever represented by counsel?' he asked.

The district attorney replied, 'I had a call today from a man who had been her counsel, and I explained the matter to him and then he returned a call and stated they were not interested in coming down and wanted the matter handled as it is being handled now.'

I can read that sentence today and weep. 'They were not interested in coming down and wanted the matter handled as it is being handled.' In plain English that meant that no one in the world was interested in looking out for me at this point.

If a woman drowns her baby, about the worst thing you can do, she's still got a right to see a lawyer, and I'd help get her one if I could.

I couldn't very well expect the Legal Aid Society to come rushing in to help a chick making a couple of thousand a week or more. I knew I was on my own. Glaser had told me this before. 'Girl,' he said, 'this is the best thing that could happen to you.'

I needed to go to a hospital and he was telling me the woodshed would be better.

So they handed me a white paper to sign. 'This is a waiver of presentation of an indictment to the Grand Jury, Miss Holiday.' They never had it so easy. I signed the second paper. The rest was up to them. I was just a pigeon.

'How do you plead?' said the clerk.

'I would like to plead guilty and be sent to a hospital,' I said.

Then the DA spoke up. 'If your Honour please, this is a case of a drug addict, but more serious, however, than most of our cases. Miss Holiday is a professional entertainer and among the higher rank as far as income is concerned. She has been in Philadelphia and appeared at the Earle Theatre, where she had a week's engagement; our agents in the Narcotics Bureau were advised from our Chicago office that she was a heroin addict and undoubtedly had heroin on her.'

'The Chicago office advised you?' the judge asked.

'That is right,' the DA replied. 'She had previously been in Chicago on an engagement. They checked and found that when she left the Earle Theatre or prepared to leave the Earle Theatre, prior to leaving she had in her possession some capsules . . . and transferred them to a man who was supposed to be her manager, named James Asundio.

'Subsequent to that, while James Asundio and Bennie Tucker were packing the bags, the agents came and identified themselves and told them why they were there, and Asundio said it was his room. They made a search of the room with his permission and found wrapped up a package, wrapped in silk lining, containing some capsules . . .

'Subsequently, Miss Holiday was apprehended in New York,' he went on. 'She has given these agents a full and complete statement and came in here last week with the booking agent (Glaser) and expressed a desire to be cured of this addiction. Very unfortunately she has had following her the worst type of parasites and leeches you can think of. We have learned that in the past three years she has earned almost a quarter of a million dollars, but last year it was $56,000 or $57,000, and she doesn't have any of that money.'

'These fellows who have been travelling with her,' this young DA continued melo-dramatically, 'would go out and get these drugs and would pay five and ten dollars and they would charge her one hundred and two hundred dollars for the same amount of drugs. It is our opinion that the best thing that can be done for her would be to put her in a hospital where she will be properly treated and perhaps cured of this addiction.'

Then the judge took over. He asked my age, if I was married, how long I'd been separated from my husband, if we had any kids, where he worked, my life story, my show-business history.

He asked me if I didn't know it was 'wrong' to have possession of narcotics. What did he expect me to say? I told him I couldn't help it after I started. Then he asked how much I used. When the federal agent Roder told him, the judge wanted to know if this was a large amount. Roder told him it was enough to kill either of them. They wouldn't be dead, they'd be damn high, that's all.

Then he wanted to know how many grains I had started with. Hell, I was no more of a pharmacist than he was. I was sick of grown men getting their kicks out of all this. They had told me if I pleaded guilty they'd send me to a hospital. I was sick and wanted to get there. This wasn't getting anyone anywhere.

I broke in and spoke to the judge. 'I'm willing to go to the hospital, your Honour,' I said.

'I know,' he said, brushing me off.

'I want the cure,' I told him.

'You stand here indicted criminally as a user of narcotics,' he said, looking me in the eye. Then the judge and the federal agents got into a long hassle which had nothing to do with me, either. The chief of the Philadelphia bureau stepped up and gave the judge a lecture on how hard they were working and said, 'I am only saying very little, if any, good will be served with their indictment and conviction other than her individual interest if we do not get some lead as to the source.'

The judge seemed to be saying they were doing me a favour. And he kept talking about an indictment and convic-tion, but there was nobody there to object.

Then the judge started on me again, asking me where I'd been on tour, who was with me, how much money I made, and where it was. This might have gone on for-ever except that somebody came in, went into a huddle with the judge. He must have been a probation officer or a social worker or something.

Then the judge lowered the boom.

'I want you to understand, as I intimated at the time of your plea, that you stand here as a criminal defendant, and while your plight is rather pitiful, we have no doubt but that you, having been nine years associated in the theatrical world, pretty well appreciate what is right – and your experiences have been many, I have been led to understand.

'I want you to know you are being com-mitted as a criminal defendant; you are not being sent to hospital alone primarily for treatment. You will get treatment, but I want you to know you stand convicted as a wrongdoer. Any other wrongdoer who has associated with you is a matter that is not for our consideration now.

'In your imprisonment you are going to find that you are going to get the very best medical treatment which can be accorded to you. That is the beneficial part of the government's position in this case.

'I do not think you have told the whole truth about your addiction at all. . . . Your commitment will depend largely on yourself, that of the supervisor and the government generally, and we hope that within the time limit in which you are to serve you will rehabilitate yourself and return to society a useful individual and take your place in the particular calling which you have chosen and in which you have been successful.

'The sentence of the court is that you

undergo imprisonment for a period of one year and one day. The Attorney General will designate the prison in which the incarceration will be made.'

People on drugs are sick people. So we end up with the government chasing sick people like they were criminals, telling doctors they can't help them, prosecuting them because they had some stuff without paying the tax, and sending them to jail.

Imagine if the government chased sick people with diabetes, put a tax on insulin and drove it into the black market, told doctors they couldn't treat them, and then caught them, prosecuted them for not paying their taxes, and then sent them to jail. If we did that, everyone would know we were crazy. Yet we do practically the same thing every day in the week to sick people hooked on drugs. The jails are full and the problem is getting worse every day.

Billie Holiday, THE LADY SINGS THE BLUES

B Imagine you spent a two-week holiday in August at the Hotel Nova in Palma Nova. Write a letter to a friend describing what it was like. Use only information obtained from the material given below and on the following page.

PALMANOVA/MAGALUF

MAJORCA

Majorca is the largest of the Balearic Islands and still is far and away the most popular holiday island in the Mediterranean. The pace of life is easy going and the scenery, especially inland, is remarkably beautiful. Towering mountain ranges overlook green, verdant valleys filled with pines; long sandy beaches are dotted with tiny, secluded, rocky coves, and sleepy villages are set amongst farmland with citrus and almond groves. There are resorts to suit every taste – from the crowded to the tranquil and the chic to the informal. In Majorca, the choice is yours!

FLIGHT DETAILS

Fly from	Flying Time (approx)
FLIGHTS TO PALMA	
Gatwick	2hrs 05mins
Luton	2hrs 20mins
Stansted	2hrs 15mins
Bristol	2hrs 15mins
Birmingham	2hrs 10mins
Manchester	2hrs 35mins
Glasgow	3hrs 45mins

All flights are weekday or weekend day or night flights.

approx. scale in miles

PALMANOVA/MAGALUF

MAJORCA

The perennial favourites of Magaluf and Palma Nova are virtual twin resorts, set beside sheltered sandy beaches on either side of a pinewooded headland about 12 miles west of Palma. Magaluf, much-loved by the young and "young at heart" is the livelier of the two: a non-stop amalgam of shops, bars, "pubs" and discothèques. Palma Nova is more family oriented, a slightly gentler world of open-air cafés, restaurants and lively nightspots. Both are linked by a regular bus service to the capital, Palma.

Transfer time from the airport: approx. 45 minutes.

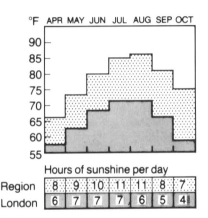

Hours of sunshine per day

	APR	MAY	JUN	JUL	AUG	SEP	OCT
Region	8	9	10	11	11	8	7
London	6	7	7	7	6	5	4

HOTEL NOVA

Position With excellent views across Palma Nova Bay, the Nova is situated in the Terranova area (the promontory between Palma Nova and Magaluf) and stands on a hillside overlooking the bay. Attractive terraces descend to the pool and its surrounding sunbathing areas, and then on to the sandy beach-style terrace. From here, the main beach is just 5 minutes away. There are shops and bars within easy walking distance.

Amenities large fresh-water pool overlooking the bay ● 'Sunset' bar ● main lounge/bar with drinks terrace overlooking the sea ● spacious sun terrace ● poolside bar – snacks available ● ladies' hairdresser ● dining-room ● hotel accepts Access, Visa and American Express credit cards.

Meals all meals are buffet-style and are served in the attractive split-level dining room ● daily change of menu and choice of main course.

Entertainment full sports/entertainments programme (daily) ● dancing to live music (twice weekly) ● English videos.

Sports tennis court ● table tennis ● sports area with volleyball.

For children separate pool ● playground ● cots ● early meals ● baby-sitting (on request locally) ● 4th bed available.

Bedrooms all twins have bath, wc, balcony ● 3rd bed available ● all singles have bath, wc, balcony.

Our opinion Spectacular views and with plenty to do, the Nova offers excellent value for money.

Board basis HB only.

Special offers no single supplement on departures up to 18/6 and in October.

Available from Gatwick, Luton, Stansted, Birmingham, Bristol, Glasgow, Manchester.

Official rating: *3-star*	**No. of rooms: *210***
No. of floors: *6*	**No. of lifts: *5***

20◆Letters

There are many different kinds of letters you might write with different purposes such as to complain, to thank, to request, to inform, to argue, and so on. You might write to many different kinds of people such as friends, relations, newspaper editors, council officials, potential employers, and so on.

Here are some points you should keep in mind.

1   The tone and the kind of language you use in letters will vary. They should be appropriate to the purpose of your letter and the person to whom you are writing. It is likely that a letter to a local figure asking him or her to present prizes at your youth club will be more formal in tone and language than a letter to a friend in which you describe that event.

2   Be direct   A letter is a means of communication between one person and another. It should be very much the same as when you speak to that person. Allow your own personality to come through and be eager to communicate. Thinking of it in this way could help you to get the tone and the language right.

3   Be clear and concise   Use simple words and sentences rather than involved complex ones. There is sometimes a danger in business and official letters of using pompous language and long sentences. Try to avoid this.

4   Keep to the subject and try to give your letter a kind of unity. In ordinary life, letters to friends and relations tend to ramble on giving any items of news that happen to come to mind. In letters of the type that might be suitable for coursework, stick to the main point and treat it as you would the description of an event or an argument but in the form of a letter.

5   Set your letter out correctly   This involves things like your address, the date, the name and address of the person to whom you are writing (in formal letters), the salutation and the ending. Look at the examples on the next page.

Formal

15 Hill Street
Fenton
Sussex
BN18 4TQ

12 September 1989

The Manager
City Bank Ltd
High Street
Manchester
M1 2TL

Dear Sir or Madam

~~~~~~

Yours faithfully

R.E. Smith

R. E. Smith

Or less formal (where you know at least the name of the person you are writing to)

15 Hill Street
Fenton
Sussex
BN18 4TQ

25 September 1989

Ms M. Shapley
City Bank Ltd
High Street
Manchester
M1 2TL

Dear Ms Shapley

~~~~~~

Yours sincerely

Roger Smith

Roger Smith

A Consider the effectiveness – or otherwise – of the tone and language used in the following letters.

1

> The text of a letter from the council of the Royal Borough of Windsor and Maidenhead to a householder who had neglected his garden.
>
> WHEREAS a hedge situated at Altwood Road, Maidenhead in Berkshire belonging to you overhangs the highway known as Altwood Road, Maidenhead aforesaid so as to endanger or obstruct the passage of pedestrians.
>
> NOW THEREFORE the Council as agent of the Berkshire County Council in pursuance of section 134 of the Highways Act 1959 hereby require you as the owner of the said hedge within fourteen days from the date of service of this notice so to lop or cut the said hedge as to remove the cause of danger or obstruction.
>
> If you fail to comply with this notice the Council may carry out the work required by this notice and may recover from you the expenses reasonably incurred by them in so doing.
>
> If you are aggrieved by the requirement of this notice you may appeal to the Magistrates' Court holden at Maidenhead aforesaid within twenty-one days from the date of the service of this notice on you.
>
> *Used in Martin Cutts and Chrissie Maher (eds),* GOBBLEDYGOOK

2 An edited version of a letter Charles Dickens wrote to *The Times* in 1849 after witnessing a public hanging.

> Sir,
>   I was a witness of the public execution at Horsemonger Lane this morning. I believe that a sight so inconceivably awful as the wickedness and levity of the immense crowd could be imagined by no man, and could be presented in no heathen land under the sun. The horrors of the gibbet and of the crime which brought the wretched murderers to it faded in my mind before the atrocious bearing, looks, and language of the assembled spectators. When I came upon the scene at midnight, the shrillness of the cries and howls that were raised from time to time, denoting that they came from a concourse of boys and girls already assembled in the

best places, made my blood run cold. As the night went on, screeching, and laughing, and yelling in strong chorus, were added to these. When the day dawned, thieves, low women, ruffians and vagabonds of every kind, flocked on to the ground, with every variety of offensive and foul behaviour. Fightings, faintings, whistlings, imitations of Punch, brutal jokes, tumultous demonstrations of indecent delight when swooning women were dragged out of the crowd by the police, with their dresses disordered, gave a new zest to the general entertainment. When the sun rose brightly – as it did – it gilded thousands upon thousands of upturned faces, so inexpressibly odious in their brutal mirth or callousness, that a man had cause to feel ashamed of the shape he wore, and to shrink from himself, as fashioned in the image of the Devil. When the two miserable creatures who attracted all this ghastly sight about them were turned quivering in the air, there was no more emotion, no more pity, no more thought that two immortal souls had gone to judgment, no more restraint in any of the previous obscenities, than if the name of Christ had never been heard in this world, and there were no belief among men but that they perished like the beasts.

I do not believe that any community can prosper where such a scene of horror and demoralization as was enacted this morning outside Horsemonger Lane Gaol is presented at the very doors of good citizens, and is passed by unknown or forgotten. And I would ask your readers to consider whether it is not a time to think of this moral evil of public execution, and to root it out.

Charles Dickens

From WRITING A LETTER, *Nelson/Post Office*

3   A letter to a local newspaper after the introduction of new 'wheelie-bins' for refuse collection.

Holding thumbs for wheelies

Dear Mr Binns (or may I call you Willy?), I feel that our daily chats on the 'phone are already leading to an on-going and promising relationship. I'll go on at you, and you'll make promises to me.

You sound so caring, and even affectionate. I can't think why other elderly folk resent being called "dear" or "love". You saw that I was elderly and unsteady on my feet. Without even demanding to have the bandages taken off you told me I'd be "put down for assistance".

"Friday's your emptying day," you explained, "and I've put you down for emptying, dear." How kind, and on one unforgettable Friday they did call – and they did empty me. Since then, alas, the flying start turned out to be a false one – and so for the last few weeks we've been having our little daily chats.

I do not like the way you answer the 'phone at once (if not before) and cheerily announce yourself: "Good morning, Willy Binns here." Then come your promises – I'm sure you don't mean to break them.

Last time we spoke I told you of an overflowing bin, and garbage littering the terrace, which is giving much pleasure to marauding squirrels and foxes and our own dogs.

Out of the kindness of your heart you said: "Tell you what I'll do. I'll come round myself, personally, this afternoon."

And you did, Willy – you did, bless your cotton gauntlets.

I welcomed you, brandishing my stick and trying to control the dogs as they rushed out.

"They won't hurt you – they know you're a friend," I assured you (sycophant that I am).

"Nice little beggars – do you breed them, dear?" you enquired.

No time to answer – for what was this? You'd brought me a second wheelie-bin and were proceeding to stuff it to over-flowing with the surplus garbage.

"But I thought you were going to empty me and take away the rubbish," I faltered.

"Can't do that, love. Different van, see. And different teams." Of course. Silly me, not to have known.

You accepted my apology and said consolingly, "You'll be all right, love. You'll be emptied on Friday. Friday's your emptying day."

Is it? Will they?

Please, Willy, see that they do and that they take away one of my wheelie bins. Two of them squatting obscenely on the terrace is just too much. I'm sorry to trouble you but I'm so afraid you'll think I want to breed them.

BARNET PRESS

B How effectively does Katherine Mansfield describe this journey in France in a letter to John Middleton Murry, a friend, dated 11 January 1918, during the First World War? How does she try to make it interesting?

My enthusiastic letter from Paris has been in my mind ever since. *And* mocked me. I took it to post; it was dark by then, piercing cold and so wet underfoot that one's feet felt like 2 walking toads. After a great deal of bother I got established in the train (no pillows to be had nowadays) and then the fun began. I liked my fellow-passengers, but God! how stiff one got and my feet hurt and the flat-iron[1] became hot enough to burn the buttoned back against which I leaned. There was no restaurant car on the train – no chance of getting anything hot – a blinding snow-storm until we reached Valence.

I must confess the country was exquisite at sunrise – exquisite – but we did not arrive at Marseilles till one o'clock. Good! As I got out a pimp getting *in* to hold a seat for some super-pimp gave me such a blow in the chest that it is blue today. I thought: 'This is Marseilles, *sans doute*.' Feeling very tired and hungry I carried my baggage 3 miles to the consigne, and finding that the train left for Bandol at 3.30 decided to have a snack at the buffet just outside – that place under a glass verandah. It was rather full, so I sat down opposite an elderly lady who eyed me so strangely that I [asked] if 'cette place est prise?' 'Non, Madame,' said she, insolent beyond everything, 'mais il y a des autre tables, n'est-ce pas? Je préfère beaucoup que vous ne venez pas ici. D'abord, j'ai déja fini mon déjeuner, et c'est très dégôutant de vous voir commencer car j'ai l'estomac délicat, et puis . . .' And then she raised her eyebrows and left it at that. You can judge what I ate after that and what I thought.

At 1.30 I went to get my baggage registered, waited for one hour in a queue for my ticket and then was told I could not have one until my passport was viséd. I had that done, waited again, carried my luggage to the platform finally at 3 o'clock *juste*, and waited there in a crowd until four. Then a train came in at another platform, and the people swarmed in just like apes climbing into bushes, and I had just thrown my rugs into it when it was stated that it was only for *permissionaires* and did not stop before Toulon. Good again! I staggered out and got into *another* train on *another* platform, asked 3 people if it was the right one, who did not know and sat down in the corner, completely dished.

There were 8 Serbian officers in the compartment with me and their 2 dogs. Never shall I say another word against Serbians. They looked like Maiden's Dreams, excessively handsome and well cared for, graceful, young, dashing, with fine teeth and eyes. But that did not matter. What *did* was that after shunting for 2 hours, five yards forward, five back, there was a free fight at the station between a mob of soldiers and the civilians. The soldiers demanded the train – and that *les civils* should evacuate it. Not with good temper, but furious – very ugly – and VILE. They banged on the windows, wrenched open the doors and threw out the people and their luggage after them. They came to our carriage, swarmed in – told the officers they too must go, and one caught hold of me as though I were a sort of packet of rugs. I never said a word for I was far too tired and vague to care about anything except I was determined not to cry – but one of the officers then let out – threw out the soldiers – said I was his wife and had been travelling with him five days – and when the *chef militaire de la gare* came, said the same – threw *him* out – banged the door, took off their dogs' leads and held the door shut. The others then pressed against the connecting door between the carriages and there we remained in a state of siege until seven o'clock when the train started. You should have heard the squalling and banging. They pinned the curtains together and I hid behind them until we were under way. By this time it was pitch dark and I knew I should never find the station as a terrific mistral was blowing and you could not hear the stations cried – but as we came to each stop they pulled the window down and shouted in their curious clipped French to know which it was. Ah, but they were very nice chaps – splendid chaps – I'll not forget them. We reached Bandol at 9. I felt that my *grande malle* was gone for ever but I seized the other 2 and dashed across the line. I could not have walked here but happily the boy from the Hotel des Bains was at the station and though he said 'qu'il n'était pas bon avec le patron', he brought me.

When I arrived the hall was rather cold and smoky. A strange woman came out, wiping her mouth with a serviette . . . I realized in a flash that the hotel had changed hands. She said she had received *no* letter – but there were plenty of rooms – and proceeded to lead me to them. My own was taken. I chose finally the one next door which had 2 beds on the condition

> that she removed one. Also it was the cheapest, 12 francs a day! The others have had *de l'eau courante* put into them and cost 13! The big stoves were not lighted in the passages . . . I asked for hot water and a hot water bottle, had some soup, wrapped up to the eyes, and simply fell into bed after finishing the brandy in my flask. For I felt that the whole affair wanted thoroughly sleeping over and not thinking about . . .
>
> 1. The burning sensation in her lung.
>
> Katherine Mansfield, THE LETTERS AND JOURNALS OF KATHERINE MANSFIELD

C Choose one of the following subjects. Use a formal tone and formal language.

1 Write a letter to someone important in the political or business worlds, expressing your approval or disapproval of something he or she has said or done.

2 Write a letter to a quality newspaper giving your views on football hooliganism, or pollution, or education.

3 Write a letter to a local business firm requesting it to sponsor your youth club in some activity.

4 The council is planning to widen the road you live in. This will involve chopping down a line of long-established trees. Write a letter of protest to the planning officer of the council.

5 Write a letter to someone you admire (perhaps in the world of sport or fashion or music) in which you express your interest in that world and ask advice on how to enter it.

D Choose one of the following subjects. Use a more informal tone and language as appropriate.

1 Imagine your family has moved to a new town. Write a letter to a friend living in the town you left describing your first impressions and reactions.

2 Imagine your brother or sister has just got married. Write a letter to a friend describing the wedding day.

3 You have received a letter from an aunt asking what you plan to do when you leave school and about your ambitions for the future. Write your reply.

4 Write a letter to a tabloid newspaper giving your views on soap operas, or violence on television, or advertising on television.

5 Write a letter to a friend in which you describe a journey you have made recently.

21 ◆ Directions, Explanations and Instructions

There could be many occasions when you have to give someone written directions, explanations or instructions. For instance, explaining to a visitor how to reach your home or your school, leaving instructions on how to deal with the burglar alarm or look after your cat when you go away on holiday, giving a friend the recipe for a favourite dish.

When writing directions, explanations and instructions, you need to keep the following in mind.

1   Use an appropriate tone   It is likely that in this kind of writing you will be objective in tone. The purpose is to give the information clearly, not to colour it with some kind of emotion or attitude.

2   Use appropriate language   Use simple vocabulary that can be easily understood, and short direct sentences.

3   Present the information clearly   Make sure you understand the sequence of events before you begin writing. Follow the sequences step by step when you write.

4   Use diagrams and annotated sketches where these would help to make what you are writing more easily understood.

5   Think about the layout of your writing and the visual effect. For instance, headings and sub-headings might help, or tabulating the points, or using a separate line for each point.

A   How effective are the directions overleaf on how to make spaghetti bolognese? Would a different kind of layout help?

There are two parts to cooking spaghetti bolognese – there is the meat sauce and then there is the spaghetti itself. To make enough meat sauce for four people you will need the following ingredients:

2 tablespoons of butter
4 tablespoons of olive oil
¼ pound of green bacon, finely chopped
1 onion, finely chopped
2 carrots, finely chopped
½ pound of minced beef
1 bay leaf
4 tablespoons of tomato purée
½ pint of beef stock
¼ pint of white wine
salt
black pepper

Heat the butter and oil in a large thick-bottomed frying pan. Add the finely-chopped bacon, onion and carrots (that is, ¼ pound of bacon, 1 onion and 2 carrots). Cook until the meat browns, stirring occasionally. Add the minced beef (½ pound), and stir continuously until it has browned evenly. Now add the bay leaf, the tomato purée (4 tablespoons), the beef stock (½ pint) and the white wine (¼ pint). Season to taste with salt and black pepper. Cover the pan and simmer gently for about half an hour. Uncover the pan and simmer for another half an hour or until the sauce has thickened.

For four people, you will need one pound of spaghetti. Fill a large pan with water, salt it and bring it to the boil. Add the spaghetti carefully. Long spaghetti should be dipped into the water a handful at a time. When this has softened slightly, it can be curled around the pan until the full length of the strand is covered. Cook the spaghetti with the lid off. Allow the water to boil briskly. Cook for about twelve to fifteen minutes, stirring frequently to prevent the spaghetti from sticking. Take out a strand of spaghetti with a fork and test. It should be tender but still firm. The Italians prefer spaghetti 'al dente' which means that it is firm enough to bite. Do not overcook the spaghetti or it becomes mushy. When ready, drain the spaghetti in a colander, making sure you remove as much water as possible. Return the drained spaghetti to the pan and add a knob of butter.

Serve the spaghetti on pre-heated plates and add the meat sauce. Sprinkle with Parmesan cheese.

B Here is a drawing of one of Heath Robinson's comic inventions. Write a serious explanation of how it works.

Anti-litter machine, from Heath Robinson, INVENTIONS

C Here is an extract from the advice given to American soldiers stationed in Great Britain during the Second World War. Some of it may sound rather strange today. Using the advice given here, draw up a list of dos and don'ts.

You are now in Great Britain as part of an Allied offensive – to meet Hitler and beat him on his own ground. For the time being you will be Britain's guest. The purpose of this guide is to start getting you acquainted with the British, their country, and their ways.

America and Britain are allies. Hitler knows that they are both powerful countries, tough and resourceful. He knows that they, with the other United Nations, mean his crushing defeat in the end.

So it is only common sense to understand that the first and major duty Hitler has given his propaganda chiefs is to separate Britain and America and spread distrust between them. If he can do that, his chance of winning *might* return. . . .

In their major ways of life the British and American people are much alike. . . . But each country has minor national characteristics which differ. . . . For instance: the British are often more reserved in conduct than we. On a small crowded island where forty-five million people live, each man learns to guard his privacy carefully – and is equally careful not to invade another man's privacy.

So if Britons sit in trains or buses without striking up conversation with you, it doesn't mean they are being haughty and unfriendly. Probably they are paying more attention to you than you think. But they don't speak to you because they don't want to appear intrusive or rude.

Another difference. The British have phrases and colloquialisms of their own that may sound funny to you. You can make just as many boners in their eyes. It isn't a good idea, for instance, to say 'bloody' in mixed company in Britain – it is one of their worst swear words. To say: 'I look like a bum' is offensive to their ears, for to the British this means that you look like your own backside; it isn't important – just a tip if you are trying to shine in polite society. . . .

When pay day comes it would be sound practice to learn to spend your money according to British standards. They consider you highly paid. . . . The British 'Tommy' is apt to be specially touchy about the difference between his wages and yours. . . .

Don't be misled by the British tendency to be soft-spoken and polite. If they need to be they can be plenty tough. The English language didn't spread across the oceans and over the mountains and jungles and swamps of the world because these people were panty-waists. . . . Britain may look a little shop-worn and grimy to you. The British people are anxious to have you know that you are not seeing their country at its best. The houses haven't been painted because factories are not making paint – they're making planes. The famous English gardens and parks are either unkempt because there are no men to take care of them, or they are being used to grow vegetables. British taxicabs look antique because Britain makes tanks for herself and Russia and hasn't time to make new cars. British trains are cold because power is needed for industry, not for heating. The trains are unwashed and grimy because men and women are needed for more important work than car-washing. The British people are anxious for you to know that in normal times Britain looks much prettier, cleaner, neater. . . .

The British of all classes are enthusiastic about sports. . . . Cricket will strike you as slow compared with American baseball, but it isn't easy to play well. . . . The big professional matches are often nothing but a private contest between the bowler (who corresponds to our pitcher) and the batsman (batter) and you have to know the fine points of the game to understand what is going on. . . . You will find that English crowds at football or cricket matches are more orderly and polite to the players than American crowds. If a fielder misses a catch at cricket, the crowd will probably take a sympathetic attitude. They will shout 'good try' even if it looks to you like a bad fumble. In America the crowd would probably shout 'take him out'. . . . You must be careful in the excitement of an English game not to shout out remarks which everyone in America would understand, but which the British might think insulting. . . .

'A short guide to Great Britain for all members of the Allied Expeditionary Forces', in Norman Longmate (ed.), THE HOME FRONT

D Choose one of the following.

1 Give directions on how to look after and care for a particular pet.

2 Explain how television, or a video recorder, or a refrigerator, or a cassette recorder works.

3 Plan the layout of your ideal school and give an explanation of your plan.

4 Prepare a leaflet on road safety or safety in the home that could be issued to junior-school children.

5 Draw up a list of fire regulations that could be used in your school.

6 Give instructions on how to make some item. It could be a piece of furniture, an article to wear, or something to eat.